COMPETING
ON VALUE

COMPETING
ON VALUE

Bridging the gap
between brand and
customer value

STAN MAKLAN

and

DR SIMON KNOX

FINANCIAL TIMES
PITMAN PUBLISHING

FINANCIAL TIMES
MANAGEMENT

LONDON · SAN FRANCISCO
KUALA LUMPUR · JOHANNESBURG

*Financial Times Management delivers the knowledge,
skills and understanding that enable students,
managers and organisations to achieve their ambitions,
whatever their needs, wherever they are.*

London Office:
128 Long Acre, London WC2E 9AN
Tel: +44 (0)171 447 2000
Fax: +44 (0)171 240 5771
Website: www.ftmanagement.com

Washington Office:
Suite 444, 1101 King Street, Alexandria, VA 22314
Tel: + 1703 519 2171
Fax: + 1703 739 6484
Website: www.ftmanagement.com

A Division of Financial Times Professional Limited

First published in the United States in 1998

The right of Simon Knox and Stan Maklan to be identified
as authors of this work has been asserted by them in accordance
with the Copyright, Designs and Patents Act 1988.

ISBN 0 273 63826 2

1 3 5 7 9 10 8 6 4 2

Typeset by Northern Phototypesetting Co Ltd, Bolton, UK
Printed and bound in the USA by
R R Donnelley & Sons

*The Publishers' policy is to use paper manufactured
from sustainable forests.*

ABOUT THE AUTHORS

Stan Maklan is a Principal Consultant with CSC Computer Sciences, one of the world's largest IT and management consulting firms, and is a regular contributor to international conferences and seminars.

He has been a director at operating companies for Unilever and Burson-Marsteller, international leaders in consumer goods and public relations respectively, as well as a marketing manager for Cable & Wireless (telecommunications). Stan has line management experience in North America, Britain and Sweden as well as experience running his own consultancy specializing in business-to-business marketing.

He was awarded honors for academic excellence when he obtained a Masters of Business Administration from the University of Western Ontario (Canada) and has a Bachelor of Science (Economics) from the Université de Montréal.

Dr Simon Knox is a Professor of Brand Marketing at the Cranfield School of Management, a leading European business school. Dr Knox is also a consultant to a number of multinational companies, including McDonald's, Levi Strauss, DiverseyLever, and the Ocean Group. Prior to joining Cranfield, Simon worked for Unilever in a number of senior marketing roles in both detergents and foods. He publishes extensively on brand equity issues and customer purchasing styles.

COMMUNICATING WITH THE AUTHORS

If you have any comments, suggestions or ideas about *Competing on Value*, please make contact with either of us.

Stan Maklan
Computer Sciences Corporation
279 Farnborough Road
Farnborough, Hants GU14 7LS, UK
Tel: + 44 (0)1252 363078
Fax: + 44 (0)1252 363992
E-mail: smaklan@cscmail.csc.com
or   stan@maklan.demon.co.uk

Simon Knox
Professor of Brand Marketing
Cranfield School of Management
Cranfield University, Cranfield
Bedford MK43 0AL, UK
Tel: + 44 (0)1234 754321
Fax: + 44 (0)1234 751806
E-mail: s.knox@cranfield.ac.uk

CONTENTS

LIST OF FIGURES

LIST OF TABLES

FOREWORD

Why did Andy Grove, CEO of a company that had maybe 50 important customers worldwide (Intel), decide to spend upwards of $150 million in television advertising for a product that few can buy directly? Why does a brand name that is synonymous with computing (IBM) find it so difficult to win favor with buyers in the personal computing market when it launched its Ambra product? And how did the first technology brand to become one of the world's top brands (Apple), an icon to marketers everywhere, fall to the point where its very survival is in question?

All these are examples from the world of technology, but that is where I have spent most of the last 25 years as a director or consultant to some of the industry's best known companies. For years this particular industry grew at staggering rates of up to 100 percent a year on the back of product-based strategies – new technologies for short periods providing a genuine unique selling proposition (USP) to their marketing focus. However, as the industry matures and product lifecycles fall to as little as 4 to 6 months, the reality of the marketing need has become clear – only having the right product is insufficient to provide a positioning and strategy which deliver sustainable, long-term competitive advantage.

Customer value, once thought to be delivered by a great product, perhaps with some acceptable support from a company whose basic brand values felt right, has moved on. No longer can product brand values succeed alone. Today, companies must recognize the need to shift from the concept of the consumer, to the understanding of the customer.

Yet so many organizations still plough millions of dollars into advertising, even into what is considered "brand" advertising without realizing that this alone, however brilliant and targetted, cannot create or deliver customer value. Advertising has its place, of course, but IBM and Apple both used to spend significant sums of money and had two of the strongest and best recognized brands in the world.

Even strong brands can be vulnerable. As the authors observe in their text, although the principle of the USP was extremely powerful and exploited mercilessly by consumer marketeers such as P&G and Unilever, the augmented brand is no longer enough. Competition can now largely copy any brand innovation whether it be product or service function or even the associated emotional "hooks." Suddenly, what was "arguably the single most important component in modern marketing practice" is becoming less effective.

At Hewlett-Packard we succeeded in extending from a company which makes products for engineers to the second largest information technology provider in the world, and the world's largest printer company with a high degree of general awareness in our target marketplaces. We have good perceived core values and competencies and yet, like many companies today, our range of businesses and corporate structure means that we do not really leverage the huge potential of our brand across all our businesses. Further, competitors can, and do, attack our markets at the product level, sometimes with more success than we would like! This is despite having one of the acknowledged best quality, process-based management systems in the world. The problem is that our competitors also have values, quality products and increasingly effective business processes.

My daily challenge, therefore, is how to create preference for our products and services and ensure delivery of the broader need for customer value. Over two-thirds of all customer defections occur because of an attitude of indifference on the part of an employee, not because of a product deficiency or competitor action. Customer loyalty is today's universal business imperative, however it is defined. My own model in Hewlett-Packard defines customer loyalty as coming from moments of truth delivering brand values through people. This critical relationship requires all the people in an organization to understand what the company core brand values are, what moments of truth they are personally involved in delivering and how they relate to the overall satisfaction and retention of customers. We are not talking just about complaints handling, customer service desks or product design. We are creating an organizational corporate planning system that will, and should, be developed to incorporate the brand management benefits which will accrue from a fully integrated customer feedback system.

However, you first have to arrive at exactly what your organization's core brand proposition should be, and determine how it will be delivered. This is where you will need UOVP – the Unique Organisation Value Proposition™ toolset, which I believe will really help. The UOVP is the first attempt I have seen to address the next step from just image or product branding. It is based on the premise that the business processes governing all company operations have to be aligned in order to deliver customer value, and many of these processes were not even apparent in the days when the traditional marketing tools were being developed. This work will provide as much a foundation for management thinking over the next five years as USP did in its time and, more importantly, is more directly impactful on business management systems and processes.

At Hewlett-Packard we were extremely fortunate to have the core values and influence of Bill Hewlett and Dave Packard (the HP Way) which still pervade the organization today. Our success stems from a real commitment to providing customers with value based on excellent products and services, being delivered through a quality-based organization, utilizing internal and external relationships all driven by our core values-based reputation. However, customer value is more and more going to be delivered through the myriad business processes within organizations which, up until now, have never been considered, nor considered themselves, to be part of brand management.

Companies need to create the imperative that forms the backbone of their corporate brand – the UOVP. It can only be delivered through the alignment of the core processes within the organization and the understanding, motivation and commitment of all the employees to manage their contribution to the customer's moments of truth. It has to be on the board agenda in order to ensure the development of that hard-to-find, differentiated positioning from which comes happy customers, staff, shareholders, communities and, last but not least, profitable growth.

Ian Ryder
Director, Brand Management and Communications
Hewlett-Packard Company
October 1997

ACKNOWLEDGMENTS

Writing a book that endeavors to move forward the theory and practice of the past 25 or 30 years is an ambitious and frightening activity. We have been fortunate and privileged in the encouragement of friends and colleagues without whom we may not have finished.

First, we must acknowledge the contribution made by Ian Ryder of Hewlett-Packard, who sat down with us over two years ago to outline the book. After a combined total of almost 60 years living with these issues, we had individually come to the conclusion that a big step forward was needed. Ian was heavily involved in the early days when the principal concept of the book, UOVP – Unique Organisation Value Proposition™, was conceived.

We wish to thank colleagues within our organizations, Cranfield School of Management and CSC Computer Sciences for all their support. Within the School, Professor Martin Christopher has been very instrumental in causing us to rethink the traditional role of brands and marketing. Catherine Bowser and Edmund Bradford, consultants with CSC, spent several extremely challenging days pushing and refining the thinking needed to develop some of the UOVP methodologies and diagnostic tools.

There were many friends and colleagues who reviewed, critiqued, and encouraged us with both practical advice and endorsement that we were on the right path. We particularly wish to thank Hugh Davidson, Chairman of Oxford Corporate Consultants and author of numerous articles and books, Andrew Seth, non-executive Chairman of The Added Value Company, Tom Blackett, Deputy Chairman of Interbrand Plc, Tony Tiernan, Marketing Director of CSC Index, John Eyre, Corporate Affairs Director of Kingfisher Plc, Larry Hochman, Director of Culture and People of AirMiles, Tonnes Funch, European Director of Motorola University, Bill Murray, Head of Managing Consulting at CSC, Louise Foerster, CSC Consulting, Bill Burgess, Senior Partner at CSC Consulting, Sue Cronizer, Shira Honigstein and Patti

Wakeling of CSC Business Research Group, and Dr David Walker of Coca-Cola whose doctoral research work at Cranfield on product brand and customer portfolio management was an inspiration to both of us.

We also owe a tremendous debt of thanks to Gill Glass at the School of Management, who managed to dispatch the very large number of jobs associated with creating this book, while remaining meticulous in her attention to every detail. We also wish to thank Mike Johnson, a colleague of many years, journalist, editor and author, for his help editing the early versions of this book.

And, finally, our dedications ...

Simon Knox wishes to thank Beatriz Ayala for her love, support and understanding.

Stan Maklan wishes to dedicate this book to his wife, Anne, and daughter, Alice, without whose help and patience it would not be possible and without whose love it would not be worthwhile.

BRAND MARKETING
IN TRANSITION

INTRODUCTION

The marketing strategies of many companies have reached a crossroads, raising questions that go to the heart of the way they think about markets, customers, channels and brands. Increasingly, companies are struggling under the pressure to add ever more value to the products and services that they sell in the face of ever-improving competition and more demanding customers. Sustainable advantage through branded products and services, the pillars of many companies' business strategy, is increasingly hard to achieve. Companies that fail to reinforce their brand pillars may find that they crumble under the relentless pressure of competition and customer demand. For many, corporate life is a treadmill of constantly squeezing time and cost out of their businesses, only to discover that customers reap all the benefits of their hard work. The future for these firms will be one of relentless reengineering, eroding margins and extreme uncertainty.

> **The marketing strategies of many companies have reached a crossroads ... Over the past ten years we have witnessed dramatic increases in competition, deregulation, customer expectations, and technology, particularly with respect to information**

The reasons are rooted in our recent history. Management consultancies and leading academics from business schools point to a unique combination of economic and commercial factors that have permanently altered the way we conduct business. Over the past ten years we have witnessed dramatic increases in competition, deregulation, customer expectations and technology, particularly with respect to information. Inflation has fallen to 30-year lows in most OECD economies and companies can no longer rely on inflated nominal profits to mask inefficiencies. This means that even to maintain existing levels of turnover and margin, companies are continually driven to add more real customer value year on year.

While today's business environment may be talked about as the toughest ever, one cannot help but suggest to business leaders that each generation faces unprecedented new challenges. Competition has increased relentlessly since World War II. Customers become more sophisticated and demanding in each decade, and technologies that we now regard as commonplace shocked the world when they were first introduced. Yet, most companies adapted to these changes and continued to prosper. How have they done this?

One of the most important adaptive mechanisms developed by companies in the post-war years has been the abil-

Brands became the focus of modern marketing practice and the heart of the adding-value process

ity to manage the demand for their goods and services. Almost 40 years ago, in a definitive article written by Harvard Business Professor Ted Levitt entitled "Marketing Myopia," compa-

nies were told to create demand for their goods and services and not merely produce to order. Levitt suggested that companies, in order to manage their revenue and profit, had to become marketing focussed and not sales or production centered. He wrote that selling is concerned with the needs of the seller, marketing addresses the needs of the customer. And so the "marketing revolution" had officially begun.

Marketing revolutionaries, like all revolutionaries, found their favorite weapon for the storming of their Bastille: the brand. For decades, strong consumer product brands and company names inspired a level of customer loyalty that enabled them to stabilize turnover while generating healthy profit margins. Many of the early brands were built as much by chance as by design. Marketers learnt from the first mass products that dominated their markets and became synonymous with their categories: Lux Soap, Kleenex, Ford, Xerox and IBM.

As business planning became more sophisticated, companies began to develop brand managers and marketing practices. Each brand manager engineered his brand to appeal to a unique segment of the market. Through advertising, ubiquitous quality and familiarity, brands became powerful business assets. Brands became the focus of modern marketing practice and the heart of the adding value process.

THE BRAND IS THE BUSINESS

In 1990 we attended a conference hosted by *The Economist* entitled "Brand is the Business." It was well attended, featuring speakers from an impressive range of world-class organizations. Each speaker related how, by embracing the most modern thinking around branding, their businesses prospered. Not surprisingly, the consumer goods industry was there, represented by Lever Europe, United Distillers and J. Walter Thompson, international leaders in consumer products, spirits and advertising. But it was not all about laundry detergents and drinks: senior executives from Hilton Hotels, ICI Fibres, Whirlpool and BP all described how they believed that in the competitive conditions of the time, their last line of defence was their brand equity.

During the 1980s the brand was king. Brand management, as a discipline, spread from its roots in consumer goods to financial services, public utilities, computing, retailing, leisure, and even industrial products. In the UK, one of the leading retail banks (Midland Bank) created product sub-brands for each different bank account it offered to customers. Telecom privatization created a brand-building bonanza in every country where competition

> **During the 1980s the brand was king**

was created. AT&T, SNET and Bell South have all hired consumer marketing professionals from the blue chip packaged goods companies. Financial services companies such as Citibank and Merrill Lynch created brand and consumer marketing organizations capable of driving more sophisticated market segmentation strategies and customer needs analysis. Computer companies began to shift their marketing emphasis from selling to IT professionals to the consumer market: Intel and Microsoft are now leading household brand names. Ralph Halpern, the dynamic 1980s' leader of Burtons, a major British clothes fashion retailer, positioned each of his retail chains to compete as brands in a specific market segment. Club Med, indeed most holiday companies, invested heavily in their brands. Every company in the 1980s claimed to be marketing led and expressed this through brand-building investments.

Brand marketers from high-quality consumer goods companies were in great demand throughout industry as company after company embraced this "marketing revolution." Brand marketing departments were established in industries where previously marketing people were developed out of engineering, project management or operational functions. Product managers replaced project engineers as the managers of new product development at Cable & Wireless. Great Britain's mail service, Royal Mail, created brand managers for first and second class mail. British Airways created a brand manager for business class (now known as Club Class). As companies recruited consumer goods marketers to fill these new roles, the Unilever-type brand-building gospel spread throughout industry.

Not only did branding become an important corporate activity, brands became valuable properties for which companies paid great fortunes. Strong consumer brand franchises were considered so impenetrable to competition, that companies wishing to expand into new markets felt it too long and expensive to build new brands from scratch. When talking to his marketing directors shortly after Unilever's acquisition of a US toiletries company, Sir Mike Perry, then head of the Personal Products group and soon to be Chairman of Unilever Plc, referred to the time and difficulty of achieving a similar presence in that key market through new brand development.

Companies with the ability to raise large sums of capital often preferred to buy leading brand properties in order to accelerate the achievement of their product portfolio and geographic expansion strategies. In the late 1980s acquisitive brand-led businesses paid very large premiums over the net asset value of companies that they acquired. While those premiums reflected the potential value of the acquired companies' distribution, customer relationships and knowhow, we maintain that the largest share of the premium went to the brands that they bought.

Table 1.1 demonstrates that in the consumer goods business, as much as 88 percent of the acquisition price was attributable to goodwill, that is the difference between the acquired company's net asset value and the price paid. In each of the examples, the acquiring company felt that it could leverage the brand equity more effectively than the acquired company and that, despite the huge premium paid for goodwill, this would be a more effective means of growing than trying to recreate the acquired company's brands on its own.

Table 1.1 Goodwill in acquisitions

Acquiring company	Acquired company	Goodwill as a % of purchase price
Grand Metropolitan	Pilsbury	88
Walt Disney	ABC	84
Nestlé	Rowntree	83
Con Agra	Beatrice	70
Cadbury Schweppes	Dr Pepper	67
United Biscuits	Verkade	66

Grand Metropolitan, which has recently merged with Guinness to form Diageo, became the first large brand-based company to capitalize this asset and declare the value attached to its brands on its balance sheet. After years of isolation in the soap makers' ghetto, brands finally made it onto the top management agenda.

OUR ICONS HAVE FALLEN

By the middle of 1994 something had gone horribly wrong. *The Economist* magazine, whose conference "The Brand is the Business" we had attended only four years before, wrote a one-page editorial questioning the future of brand marketing. What had occurred in a mere four years?

The cause of *The Economist*'s angst was the Friday, April 2 1993 announcement by the Philip Morris Company of the need for a large price reduction on its flagship Marlboro brand to stem the flight of customers to lower priced brands. Following that announcement on what is now termed "Black Friday," the company lost $20 billion in market value as its share price plunged. The market had realized that even the strongest consumer brands could no longer command customer loyalty and high margins. While it is true that over subsequent years Marlboro has recaptured much of its lost share, the senior management view of brands' ability to add value had begun to turn around.

The news for brands did not get any better as the 1990s unfolded. One brand icon after another was knocked off its pedestal. Companies that had paid huge premiums to buy brands found their investments worth far less than had been paid for them.

In 1995 Coca-Cola's UK brand share temporarily slipped below 50 percent for the first time in its history following the activities of retailer brands and an innovative third party manufacturer (Cott Cola) that allied with Virgin and Tesco (Britain's leading food retailer). In the leading supermarket chains, such as Tesco or Sainsbury, Coke is not always the category leader. Retailers' own brands have successfully extended into a category long dominated by advertising-led brands. Like Marlboro, Coke has regained its lost share, but at tremendous cost. Coke's advertising budget is reported to have increased twelve-fold following the launch of Virgin Cola and Sainsbury's Classic Cola. Its pricing policy now reflects retailer brands' prices. Even Coca-Cola, one of the world's leading brands, cannot fully determine its own pricing and margin. While retailers' own brands hold a much smaller share of marketing in the USA, Cott Corporation, the leading third-party cola bottler, grew ahead of the industry average for much of the 1990s. Cott's success prompted its much larger branded competitors to launch a vicioius price war. This price war has undoubtedly limited the penetration of retailer brand colas in the USA, but it has been at a cost.

In Britain, oil giants such as Shell, BP and Exxon have lost 25 percent of the UK gasoline market to British food retailers' own brands in just a few years. Per outlet, food retailers are outselling the traditional gasoline market leaders by a ratio of at least 6:1. With the recent extension of retailers' loyalty bonus points to the gasoline that they sell, their market share is likely to rise further. The traditional brand leaders have responded with massive investments on all fronts: forecourt food stores, new facias, advertising and price reductions. A sign of the times is when a major gasoline brand leader has posted a sign claiming that its gasoline is sold "at grocery store prices" at a station off one of Europe's busiest motorways. Who can argue that, in the UK at least, price leadership has been lost by what was one of the world's most powerful oligopolies. One hundred years of brand leadership, universal awareness and massive investments in advertising are not enough to create customer loyalty and preference. The consumer of the 1990s is not willing to pay a price premium for gasoline.

IBM, Digital and Apple, the three largest personal computer brands in the world during the 1980s, found themselves struggling to survive in that market in the 1990s. IBM's response to the low-end PC market in the 1990s, the Ambra brand, was withdrawn from the market shortly after launch. Marketing consultants in the 1980s held Apple up to their clients as an example of how branding could create fanatical loyalty in that market. At the time of writing, Apple's future as an independent company is being questioned. Digital had retreated from positioning itself as a full-range, IBM-like supplier, into a series of high-value niches, such as new microchip technology. Newer, lower cost and more innovative PC builders such as Compaq, Dell and Gateway grew to dominate this market. In the ultimate twist to the story, at the time of writing, Compaq announced its purchase of Digital. Even in a high-risk purchase such as computers, established brand leaders cannot achieve premium prices for me-too product performance.

Even McDonald's is not immune. In response to slumping sales early in 1997, Jack Greenberg, head of US operations, made an urgent plea to franchisees to reduce the price of a Big Mac from $1.90 to 55 cents with the purchase of fries and a drink – a reduction of over 70 percent.

Long-established names in the business services industry have witnessed decades of hard work and good reputation swept aside by acquisitive companies such as ASEA Brown Boveri and BTR. These empire builders offer a stark choice for many individual companies: sell out or become irrelevant. In many industries, the pressures of international supply chains are forcing mergers and alignments that are reducing the number of company brands in any one market.

Empire builders offer a stark choice for many individual companies: sell out or become irrelevant

Andrex, Britain's toilet paper market leader, seemed to defy gravity in the 1980s. While low-priced toilet paper overtook market leaders in country after country, the British remained Andrex loyal. Marketers ascribed this feat to the emotional values wrapped into the brand through its advertising symbol, the Andrex puppy. For many years,

Andrex has been a case study in the power of brands. The long serving advertising agency, JWT, was enormously proud of this advertising/brand property. But since 1990 the brand has lost one-third of its market share and in October 1996, Kimberly Clark, the new owners of Andrex, announced the severing of the brand's long association with JWT and the search for new advertising magic.

Throughout the 1990s one seemingly unassailable leading brand after another has been found wanting by increasingly more demanding customers. Habit, familiarity and reassurance alone did not stem the tide of defections from products or companies that failed to offer the best customer value in their market.

The best mass marketers of consumer goods are responding through ruthless product portfolio rationalization ("core brand strategy"), elimination of non-value added costs, increased investment in product quality, increased advertising behind core brands and a reduced price premium to credible, lower priced competitors. This sensible and overdue brand husbandry is helping brand leaders, particularly in America, to rebound from the recession of the early 1990s and consolidate strong positions in developed economies while investing for growth in Asia and Eastern Europe.

Some have suggested that strong branded products have met the challenge of recessionary times and beaten back competition. We suggest however, that the last recession has merely exposed irreversible changes in the way consumers interact with brands. Indeed, in many

> *Habit, familiarity and reassurance alone did not stem the tide of defections from products or companies that failed to offer the best customer value in their market*

industries even good brand husbandry has not stabilized prices or consumer loyalty. In the UK even well managed consumer brands have not reversed retailers' own-label share gains.

Increased competition, rapid product development cycles, faster imitation of innovation, more sophisticated channel partners and more empowered customers have ended the days when sustainable advantage could be secured through product brands and services alone. Companies must leverage a broader range of assets, business processes and relationships to compete successfully through the value chain.

The future will put even more pressure on the way in which traditional product brand leaders compete. Media fragmentation is set to explode in the 21st century around the world, making it increasingly expensive to build brands through the mass media. In 1997, there were almost 1600 television stations in the USA, almost twice as many as in 1970. Cable TV systems numbered almost 11,000 and there were 10,300 commercial radio stations. A colleague posted to Japan commented that he could receive over 400 radio stations from his home in Yokohama. In Europe, deregulation of the mass media is allowing choice to expand.

In addition to increased choice of traditional media, the Internet is capturing an increasing amount of individual's "share of screen-time." The emergence of the Internet is akin to that of television after World War II. It will not only become an important new medium, it will fundamentally impact the relationship between buyer and seller in a way that will disadvantage traditional stand-alone product brands.

Customer loyalty will be even harder to maintain as the information age further empowers customers and leading companies deploy, and improve upon, highly sophisticated relationship marketing systems that they are currently developing.

Finally, we predict that in the future the customer will direct the value chains in which they operate. We are already seeing consumers aligning to retailers and entering into a virtual long-term supply partnership with them. "Where you shop becomes more important than what you buy," claims Robert Bailey, Heinz UK's Marketing Director. Information technology will enable customers to go even further in dictating to the market how they wish to be served. Larry Hochman, a director of AirMiles, suggests that in the future, the role of the front-line service employee will be to empower customers and not simply to process enquiries and solve problems. Reconfigured value chains, directed by information empowered customers, will challenge every-one's right to brand.

SUMMARY

The cornerstone of many companies' marketing strategy is to develop loyal customers willing to pay premium prices for branded goods and services. Throughout the 1980s branding moved from its ghetto in the consumer goods industry to the mainstream of business activity. Companies in almost every industry invested heavily in building brands for their products, services and companies.

By the mid-1990s it had become apparent that the investment in creating a brand was no longer a guarantee of long-term and defensible advantage in the marketplace. One famous brand after another found that it could no longer command strong price pre-miums to their competitors nor expect the automatic loyalty of its customers.

This shift in customer behavior and attitude toward brands did not reverse itself, as many had predicted, when the recession of the early 1990s ended. Looking into the future, we predict that the spread of powerful new information technologies will further empower customers to extract ever-increasing levels of value from their suppliers. The attack on the ability of product alone to create customer loyalty and premium prices will only intensify.

Further reading

We have found that the best descriptions of the crisis facing the brand are to be found in the press and not in marketing textbooks.

Alan Mitchell, a British journalist with columns in a number of UK publications, has been following the leading edge of brand theory for a number of years and Professor Knox has published on the issues facing the traditional product brand.

- Ted Levitt, "Marketing Myopia," *Harvard Business Review*, July–August 1960.

For a definitive text on brand management and classical brand marketing, see David Aaker's book, *Building Strong Brands*. The power of branding in an American context is made clear.

- David Aaker, *Building Strong Brands*, Free Press, New York, 1996.

Brands on the balance sheet has been debated, on and off for over 15 years. The pros and cons of this debate have been presented by Patrick Barwise and colleagues.

- Patrick Barwise, J.A. Likierman and P.R. Marsh, *Accounting for Brands*, Institute of Chartered Accountants in England and Wales, London, 1989.

The *Economist* article that appeared in the wake of Marlboro Friday is recommended as it remains a sounding bell for business managers.

- Anon, "Death of the Brand Manager," *The Economist*, April 9 1994.

THE VALUE GAP

INTRODUCTION

Brands have got into trouble where a gap has developed between customer value and brand value. Marketing has been focused on creating brand value, particularly in the brand-conscious eighties, rather than exploring customer value and translating this into a value proposition through branding. Prices of many consumer brands rose faster than raw material inflation, and the cost of advertising rose faster than the prices of many other factors of brand production. In the meantime, quality levels rose across the board in most industries, customers became more discerning and knowledgeable, and choice increased dramatically. The

> **Brands have got into trouble where a gap has developed between customer value and brand value**

recession of the 1990s has probably encouraged customers to take a hard look at the value of all their purchases, thus exposing the weaknesses of many brand leaders.

THE VALUE OF BRANDS

The brand does not describe the product, it distinguishes it. Brands were seen to be of economic value to their owners through their ability to differentiate products and services from competitive offers that were, in reality, rather similar. This differentiation was achieved by convincing prospective customers that there was something of added value in one's brand that made it more attractive, even at a premium, compared to lower priced competitors. Brand marketing is constantly looking for ways to add real value to the basic service or product in order to create brand preference and loyalty.

> **The brand does not describe the product, it distinguishes it**

THE VALUE OF INFORMATION AND RISK

Another way of looking at branding is to suggest that brands provided information that made it easier for customers to decide to buy. When faced with a purchase, the consumer or industrial buyer's problem is risk: will the product perform in use or will it signal the wrong things about me as a person or company?

The performance risk in any purchase is the consequence of the product or service failing to provide its basic functional benefits. It could be the car that breaks down, the pen that fails to write, the software program that crashes or the defective component that shuts down a factory production line.

Psychological risk is associated with how customers think others will perceive them as a result of their purchase choice. This psychological risk is thought to be a part of every purchase decision but is probably best illustrated in the automotive market where one worries about the image one creates through the brand of car driven. Clothes, toiletries, and even choice of grocer, all contain an element of psychological risk. The business market is not immune to it and we have all heard of the now-dated expression, "You never get fired for choosing IBM."

The early era of brand building focused on helping customers manage performance risk. Added value was often achieved through claims around the core functionality of products: "washes whiter," "new improved," "now with added ingredient x," "lower tar and nicotine," "more instructions per second," "faster hard disk access," etc.

As product technology became available to an ever-increasing number of competitors, there were fewer and fewer motivating product claims to make. Claims around the core functionality of products and services became less and less relevant to customers and harder to defend against competitors' claims. One calorie per can of

Coke or one milligram of tar per cigarette and fat-free milk all reached their technical limit. Clothes were as white as we could perceive them to be, music reproduction exceeded our ears' ability to differentiate, and several million instructions per second became increasingly irrelevant to computer users.

THE AUGMENTED BRAND

In response, brand marketers shifted their emphasis to adding value beyond the core functionality of the product or service. The focus moved to the creation of layers of added value surrounding this core functionality in order to distinguish the brand from competitors with similar performance characteristics. In particular, marketing looked to managing psychological risk: enhancing a person's sense of well-being and accomplishment through the things that they buy. Image had always been a part of branding but by the early 1980s, professional marketers learned the formula for building and extending emotional values into products and services.

The soap makers jettisoned "washes whiter" advertising and instead went for cuddly teddy bears, caring mothers, puppies and fairytale princesses. Emotional reasons to buy supplemented core functionality as the critical value adding elements of the brand proposition. At Unilever, brand psychologists replaced scientists as the drivers of added value.

In a similar vein, telephone companies do not merely provide connectivity, they are an agent for improved social interaction, closer families and international co-operation. The energy providers do not just sell you gas, electricity or

> *At Unilever, brand psychologists replaced scientists as the drivers of added value*

nuclear power: they are creating exports, wealth, scientific progress and environmental clean-up.

Telecommunications companies around the world have shifted their advertising campaigns from what we would describe as generic telephone calls to friends and relatives abroad toward the notion that communication adds value to society. British Telecom's tag line, "It's good to talk," is intended to be about relationships between people, maintaining contact with friends and stronger family ties all facilitated by low-cost telephony. Bell Atlantic's tag line, "Bringing people together," is a further example of this trend.

The American Automobile Association (AAA) recently changed its name to the AAA Member Network in a move designed to broaden its brand position in travel and financial services. It is already a leading travel agency and insurer and has announced that it will provide full service banking to its members. Its new advertising theme is "travel with someone you trust," reflecting its bigger emotional appeal than just roadside recovery. Around the same time, Britains' equivalent organization, the AA, began advertising itself as the country's fourth emergency service after the police, fire and ambulance services. The brand is making an even more ambitious emotional jump from roadside assistance to that of a national institution.

Management consultancies no longer only provide counsel and analysis, they are academic institutions advancing mankind's knowledge of and ability to manage organizations. McKinsey is reported to spend $50 million per annum on management research and publishing while CSC Index has co-authored two bestselling management books, *Reengineering the Corporation* and *The Discipline of Market Leaders*. The former sold over 2 million copies.

It is not only in the area of psychological benefit where companies create new forms of added value and differentiation for their product brands. Some airlines provide transportation to and from the airport for important customers, to offer them more of an end-to-end service. Freight forwarders provide logistics support so that their services can compete on a basis other than lowest cost. Industrial component makers offer engineering services so that their companies are seen to provide more than merely parts.

Another form of adding value is by making it easy to buy or obtain – this we term "ubiquity of presence." The classic example of adding value through ubiquity is Coca-Cola, a brand that strives to be within arm's reach of desire. A home delivery pizza company in Toronto grew by advertising its telephone number in a memorable tune and not by talking about its

> *The classic example of adding value through ubiquity is Coca-Cola, a brand that strives to be within arm's reach of desire*

products or Italian heritage – the pizza was always within a telephone's reach.

Leading writers on the subject of marketing have explained this movement, from core functionality to presence through the other layers of added value, in terms of the "augmented brand." In many

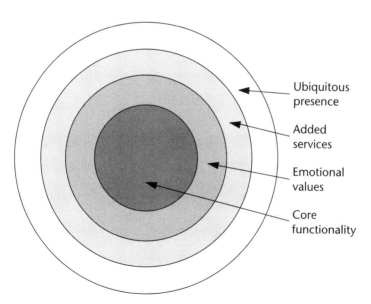

Ubiquitous presence

Added services

Emotional values

Core functionality

Fig. 2.1 The augmented brand

marketing texts, this is illustrated by the concept of concentric circles expanding out from the core product benefits. These "augmented brand" layers comprise emotional values, services and ubiquity of presence or ease of access to the product (see Fig. 2.1).

THE UNIQUE SELLING PROPOSITION

While the augmented brand is often necessary for the creation of a powerful brand, it is not sufficient. Competitors are quick to copy successful brand innovations either in core functionality, added value services or the emotional wrap-around. In the grocery business, retailers can copy brand innovations in a matter of weeks and introduce them at lower cost. The augmented brand became a powerful corporate asset only through effective differentiation between one brand and another.

This critical differentiation has traditionally been achieved through the development of the unique selling proposition (USP), arguably the single most important component of modern branding practice. The USP is a succinct statement about the brand's most important customer benefit together with the supporting evidence, either psychological or functional.

In practice, the USP is a one-sentence distillation of why the customer will buy your brand and not the competitor's. This proposition can obviously arise from a clear-cut technical benefit of relevance to the prospective customer: the marketer's equivalent of nirvana. A discount retailer will advertise lower prices while the higher priced department store will talk about its range of quality products and the overall convenience of the shopping experience. One brand of laundry detergent will claim to be the most efficacious product for stains and heavily soiled clothes while its competitors will take the high ground in other claim areas, such as whiteness and freshness.

Over time, functional differentiation becomes increasingly difficult because competitors get better. The marketer increasingly looks for a USP in the emotional value added layer of the brand, as that portion of the augmented brand is thought to be hardest to imitate. Marlboro takes refuge in its image of American masculinity. Volvo positions itself along the dimension of safety. Apple computers were the choice of rebels and non-conformists. Against Procter & Gamble's Ariel laundry detergent, Unilever positions Persil as part of motherly care: Unilever pits Persil's emotional values against Ariel's efficacy image.

The USP is a highly effective means of differentiation because it is information efficient: one only needs to educate the market to remember one key message or fact. At its best, the USP is translatable into a mnemonic device or slogan that is permanently and universally remembered and the brand is permanently differentiated from its competitors:

- Apple computer, the computer for the rest of us
- Timex watches – takes a lickin' and keeps on tickin'
- It's Miller time
- This Bud's for you
- You always have room for Jell-O
- A Mars a day helps you work, rest and play.

4Ps MARKETING

The USP was executed through the 4Ps of marketing made famous by Professor Philip Kotler in the late 1960s: product, price, promotion, place. The product is generally considered to include the packaging and promotion to include advertising. Marketing's task was to create a coherent set of policies for each of the Ps in consideration of its brand's USP. In addition to the advertising (promotion) just discussed, marketing would ensure that the price was consistent with the USP, the packaging conveyed a similar message and the product was sold in the right places. A "high-tech" skin cream such as those from Laboratoires Garnier (a division of L'Oréal) will make strong beauty claims in its advertising, be sold in exclusive shops, at high prices and be elegantly packaged. As Charles Revson, founder of one of the world's premier cosmetics companies, said, "In the factory we make skin cream, in the store we sell hope." However, Vaseline skin cream has a more functional advertising message around dry hands, is sold at mass market prices in groceries and drugstores and has ordinary, convenient packaging. The 4Ps were manipulated to reinforce the USP determined by marketers. Good marketing manages every moment of customer contact with the brand to reinforce the brand's USP.

Over time the marketing community's knowledge of the effect of various stimuli on customer perceptions was extensive. Brand managers became brand engineers, manipulating well-tried stimuli to achieve predictable results.

BRAND MANAGEMENT

As we have already seen, it was not only brands and their augmented value that created value for companies. The brand management system itself represented a highly effective organizational design for managing product innovation, change and consumer needs.

Procter & Gamble is widely credited with inventing the concept of "one-man-one-brand" in the 1930s, some 50 years after it launched Ivory Soap in the USA. P&G found that as its product brand portfolio increased, traditional functional management could no longer handle the complexity of the product portfolio. It decided to break the company into mini-companies centered around the product brands that created consumer value. Each major brand would be run by its own brand manager / brand office that would be responsible for marketing, advertising, pricing, promotion, packaging and innovation. Central management would run functions for which there were clear economies of scale including manufacturing, warehousing, sales, finance and personnel.

This system allowed even the biggest of companies to remain entrepreneurial and fast moving. Young brand managers took no prisoners: they relentlessly analyzed consumer needs and competitive weaknesses to bring innovation to the market ahead of rivals. Brand managers were even encouraged to compete with their colleagues within P&G: no brand would escape the discipline of full competition.

Decision making was decentralized and taken by people with their fingers on the pulse of the market. Brand managers would prove themselves on ever-larger and more complex brands and this ensured that the most able directed P&G's key brand properties. Young men became mini-CEOs quickly and P&G had an inexhaustible supply of talented general managers from which to groom senior executives.

The system proved so successful that every major consumer marketing organization has since copied it. The system has extended successfully into many other industries such as telecommunications, computing, retailing and banking.

MAKING MONEY FROM BRANDS

Sustained advertising and publicity behind a meaningful and customer-relevant USP can create a permanent positioning and awareness among customers. Once the USP enters into the customer's subconscious, at each event that drives purchase, the psychological script is played back and the customer considers the brand. The augmented brand, coupled with the USP, become powerful tools for building turnover at higher prices to less desirable brands.

Brands became permanent icons of the consumer society and enduring symbols of value and quality. Table 2.1 demonstrates that consumer brand leaders of the 1940s remained the brand leaders 50 years later, defying the product lifecycle theory of marketing. It seemed as if well-maintained brands would endure forever, generating huge profits for brand owners through the future.

Table 2.1 US brand leaders, 1947 and 1997

Category	1947 leader	1997 position
Soft drinks	Coca-Cola	Number 1
Razors	Gillette	Number 1
Film	Kodak	Number 1
Breakfast cereal	Kellogg's	Number 1
Vacuum cleaners	Hoover	Number 1

Source: Saatchi & Saatchi and A.C. Nielsen

While it is the brand that created this value in consumer markets, it was the advertising that created the brand. Beer, a category in which companies invest millions in branding, is a case in point. An executive at JWT once said, "The consumer drinks the advertising, not the beer." Telecom companies have developed sophisticated tracking systems that can associate advertising expenditure with call revenue generation. Branding is far more than advertising, but mass advertising certainly provided the communications infrastructure needed to create mass brands.

Some business-to-business marketers have successfully adopted the practice of consumer branding to create preference for their organization and accelerate their rate of growth. In 1989 Andersen Consulting decided that its growth was inhibited by its being perceived merely as a division of its tax and auditing parent, Arthur Andersen. The consulting management structure was spun off and repositioned itself in the expanding IT-led, change management marketplace. Part of this investment was in the largest ever business services advertising campaign. It was the first time that a management consultancy used television advertising, albeit well targeted, to sell multimillion-dollar services. Within five years of this investment, Andersen Consulting's turnover increased from just over $800 million to $2.5 billion.

THE LINK IS SEVERED

By the 1990s, however, the link between brand building and value creation was not so clear. Traditional product branding, based upon the USP and the augmented brand, was no longer generating sufficient levels of added value to increase customer loyalty and market demand. As a result, we are witnessing the growth of a gap between brand value and customer value, the latter stemming increasingly from processes outside the remit of traditional product brands and brand management. There has been a dramatic change in customer purchase processes which calls into question the traditional link between brand and customer value.

Widely acknowledged as having the most powerful brand in the computer industry since the late 1970s, Apple Computer failed to beat the then almost unbranded competition through the 1980s (Compaq, Dell, Gateway). People warmed to Apple but bought competitors' products because of operating system standards, Apple's restrictive distribution practices and higher prices.

Mercury Communications modeled its challenge to British

Telecommunications (BT) on Virgin's successful positioning against British Airways. It created highly memorable and likable advertising through the use of a popular British comedian. However, 13 years after the creation of Mercury as Britain's alternative phone company, Cable & Wireless (the holding company) is starting all over again and rebranding a reconstructed Mercury. The emotional value added of the brand was unable to sustain customer recruitment after BT had improved its service and reduced its prices in response.

Even more worrying for the advocates of traditional branding is the inescapable fact that many recent consumer goods marketing successes have not been advertising led. The traditional approach to building a new brand was to establish awareness and interest through advertising an interesting proposition, while building trial through coupons and in-store promotion. Repeat purchase and loyalty were expected to follow automatically if the product did not disappoint.

Snapple began large-scale advertising only after it had achieved a critical mass. Its advertising featured responses to real consumer letters that were coming into the company. For Snapple, it was more important at the outset to gain distributioin with the right retailers, than to invest in advertising.

The Body Shop successfully entered the fiercely competitive US health and beauty care market much more on the basis of a radically different and compelling consumer proposition than on advertising-generated awareness and interest. While we believe the Body Shop is excellent at generating free publicity through its causes, Anita Roddick, co-founder, publicly eschews advertising as inappropriate and wasteful.

Häagen-Dazs ice cream established itself in Europe prior to commencing advertising. In comparison to other food products, the brand is lightly advertised. Müller yogurt, a leading German brand, successfully entered the well-established UK market with limited advertising but quickly grew to become the leading branded product in its category. By way of contrast, the French market leader, Danone, entered the UK market around the same time that Müller began its brand-building drive. Danone followed the more traditional entry strategy of supporting its new product launch with high levels of advertising and publicity but failed to maintain its initial success and shelf presence. The category of yogurt that Danone virtually created in the UK is now dominated by retailers' own brands.

More often than not, advertising is not the basis for brand building.

The value of the brand, traditionally its ability to mitigate performance and psychological risk, has eroded. Risk is no longer the customer's prime problem. The customer can, in most markets, choose between a large number of high-quality products made by renowned companies. In the modern economy, value is no longer exclusively created by marketers branding what their employers wish to produce, rather it is created by the affiliation of customers with trusted suppliers; value creation is anchored in customers' need for supply partnerships that deliver value over a period of time.

> *The value of the brand, traditionally its ability to mitigate performance and psychological risk, has eroded*

Instead of the augmented brand and the USP, customers are looking for:

- relevant information and not sales pitches
- secure supplies over time and not unrelated one-off transactions
- customization and not meaningless choice
- a true relationship with their suppliers and not mere cross-selling.

These components of customer value are discussed in detail in the remainder of the chapter.

COMPONENTS OF CUSTOMER VALUE

Information, not sales pitches

Customers are highly sophisticated and confident in their own ability to decide between products and suppliers' offers; they need much less brand reassurance to validate their choices.

Customers have access to more and more information about products, competitors, guarantees, etc. and are making more informed decisions: they know the questions to ask, what are fair prices and what level of after-sales support they can expect. For example, many supermarkets now post the price per pound or ounce at their shelf displays. This helps the consumer understand the price advantage of competing brands, especially own-brands.

Price premiums need to be justified by more than a label in today's market

The post-war generation has grown up in a consumer society and is highly experienced at decision making in competitive markets; customers are better judges of risk and need less brand reassurance to mitigate it.

Competition has driven quality standards to the point where it is becoming rare to find a great disparity in manufacturing standards for similar products. Privately, major automobile makers will say that there is little to choose between cars of a similar price. Retailers' own-label products are generally as good as those from the traditional product brand leader. Consumer electronics from new Asian competitors are at least as good as those from the traditional market leaders. Product and service innovation and quality is readily imitable by competitors. It is increasingly difficult to compete on product quality and functionality alone.

In the post-1980s boom period conspicuous brand consumption is less attractive. In the 1980s new companies introduced us to designer cookies, underwear, stationery, glasses and baby clothes.

The specialist retailer took share from the mass marketer. In the 1990s the trend has reversed with Marks & Spencer and The Gap taking share from prestige retail brands. Many luxury brands have had to cut prices in order to survive. Price premiums need to be justified by more than a label in today's market.

We conclude that, in some markets, there is a permanent reduction in the amount of performance and psychological risk associated with the buying decision in both consumer and business markets. Where this is so, one of the attributes of brands, the ability to help customers manage risk, is weakened and traditional branding is less effective than it once was.

In a number of consumer goods markets, brands can no longer command premium prices or even shelf space by virtue of their advertising-generated awareness alone: performance must justify the price and place. This has created a permanent reduction in the value of many consumer goods brands.

Relationships, not transactions

For this new world, customer value is increasingly created through a relationship with a supplier for a stream of goods and services over time. Purchasing is moving from being a specific event in time to a mutual commitment between supplier and customer.

Traditional product brands, with their in-built bias toward adding levels of value upon functionality, features and attributes, fail to offer customers the type of relationship that engenders brand loyalty. In the UK, for example, consumers are increasingly committed to their relationship with their grocer and its loyalty scheme more than they are to any individual brand of laundry detergent, shampoo or prepared meals. Traditional product brands are, to quote McKinsey & Co., losing their "right to brand" to the new value chain leaders.

Relationship-based marketing has always been a major component of the business-to-business brand. Industrial component suppliers compete on their ability to supply the right product, at the right time, and at the right place, consistently and reliably. The cost of factory downtime is more important than minor enhancements in function and features of the component itself. The benefits of co-operation, co-engineering and just-in-time supply chain outweigh cost considerations alone. Customer value in business-to-business markets has long been relationship based.

Purchasing is moving from being a specific event in time to a mutual commitment between supplier and customer

---

The concept of the relationship has been used by business marketers. Ironically, IBM was one of the first companies to understand this. At its most successful, IBM did not offer customers merely the best product functionality or value for money – IBM became your computing partner and helped you develop and run systems. Suddenly, in the 1990s, its role in this regard was largely overtaken by the biggest IT services companies such as Andersen Consulting, CSC and EDS, each of which brands itself with characteristics that feature strategic alliance, outsourcing and partnership.

Relationship-based competition has moved into the mass consumer market. Modern work practices, facilitated by ever more powerful desktop computing, have enabled companies with even the largest customer bases to provide a level of individual service and customization. Telephone banking companies provide greater customer convenience, and should be able to offer services at lower cost than traditional banks. Air travel and grocer loyalty schemes can reward individual customers for exhibiting desired purchasing behavior. Frontline service people at British Airways provide a full service 24 hours a day, only the accent of the person changes during the course of the day as the computer systems switch support from

London to New York to Hong Kong. Airlines keep a record of customers' preferred seating, meals and travel arrangements to anticipate their needs. As all the major carriers begin to offer similar quality of flights, one chooses the carrier that one knows and serves one best. Jan Carlzon, former head of SAS Airlines, correctly foretold the coming customer service revolution in his industry 15 years ago when he stated that "the battle for the skies will be won on the ground."

The fastest growing consumer markets also require a much larger degree of counselling and systems integration than ever. Computers, mobile telephones, interactive television and software suppliers add more value to customers when they maintain ongoing support and product upgrade service. For a number of years leading computer experts have published research claiming that as much as 80 percent of the total cost of owning a computer is in the servicing, upgrading and problem solving. The discriminator between personal computers increasingly is in their level of after-sales support, while consumers believe that each offers roughly equivalent product specification and functionality.

Car companies have realized this and have made major investments in their dealer network's ability to provide after-sales service. One does not just buy a car, one buys mobility. That mobility is guaranteed both by the maker's reputation for quality and a relationship with the dealer for a number of years into the future. Poor after-sales service is the surest way to spoil a car manufacturer's brand name.

Marks & Spencer continually changes its range of prepared meals to offer novelty and interest. The value added of this retailer is not in the product *per se*, but the fact that one can visit regularly and be guaranteed interesting new recipes. The market leading product brands such as those offered by Findus (part of Nestlé) or Bird's Eye Walls (Unilever), find it difficult to deliver the same value. The way these companies go to market through their cycle of market research, development, mass production, mass distribution, and advertising support precludes the continuous innovation of a Marks & Spencer. Findus and Bird's Eye Walls create powerful product brands, Marks & Spencer created a powerful supply chain management system that adds more value for its customers than product brands can reasonably hope to do.

Customization, not choice

In 1995 a senior executive of CSC declared to his major retailer clients that customer choice was dead. He stated that the bewildering choice of products and services that suppliers offered consumers over the past 20 years was the outgrowth of the failed experiment of the 1970s and 1980s. Customers do not want choice, they want what they want. Companies create customer value by helping their customers decide what solution is best, and then by producing to order, in good time, and at a competitive price.

Brand-based competition encourages suppliers to offer ever more choice of slightly differentiated products and their line extensions. Ten years ago, there were over 600 brands of shampoo on the American market and today there are over 200 different toothpaste lines in the UK. Marketers are bombarding consumers with innumerable choices and decisions in every aspect of life: groceries, toiletries, reading, public utilities, financial services, and recreation. The consumer problem of the 1990s is not product quality or even customer service, it is merely coping with the number of decisions available.

The net result is that this bewildering array of slightly differentiated brands in every category does not necessarily create value. It creates confusion for customers and tremendous cost inefficiencies throughout the supply chain. However, product brand managers cannot allow their competitors to edge ahead in the battle for functionality and features, shelf space, promotional activity, and the like. Traditional product brand management is more concerned with competition than customer value creation.

> *The consumer problem of the 1990s is not product quality or even customer service, it is merely coping with the number of decisions available*

Today, businesses and consumers are coping with choice by selecting key partners with whom they will enter into relationships for large portions of their supply needs. Variants of the following homily from the car industry are often mentioned in marketing texts:

> In the beginning of the mass market, you could have any color car, as long as it was black. The next stage was to offer you a limited choice of colors from which you selected your preference. The next stage from that was to ask you to tell us the color you wanted. Now we sit down to discuss the role of color in your car selection process.

Supply partnerships are a well-established policy in virtually every industrial sector. Car companies no longer wish to deal with thousands of component suppliers. Instead, a few dozen are contracted to be strategic partners for various sub-assemblies, such as braking systems. Power plant builders sub-contract for sub-assemblies, such as electrical systems or pipeworks. These relationships are characterized by strong interaction between organizations at all levels to specify what is needed and then cooperate to produce it in a timely and cost-effective pattern.

Consumer marketers are following suit. Many retailers will only stock the number one and two brands in addition to their own label in a given category. Unilever's chairman, Niall Fitzgerald, has announced that the company will discontinue or sell off 25 percent of the brands that it markets in order to concentrate on core brands. Procter & Gamble is leading a public debate in the detergent business for manufacturers to reduce the number of sizes offered.

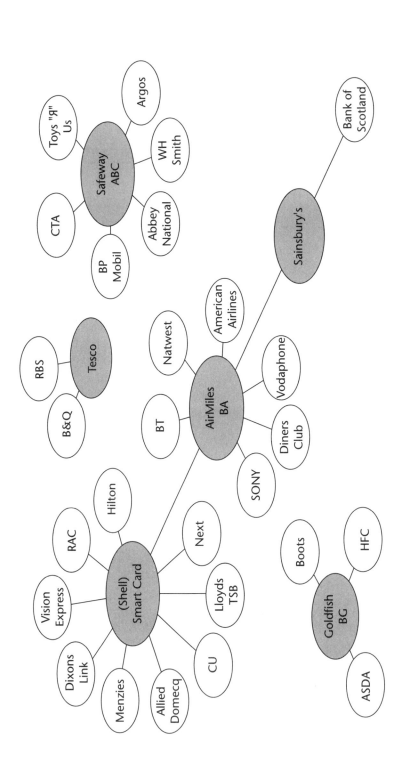

Source: Maklan, CSC, April 1997

Fig. 2.2 UK consumer loyalty network

Part of the value proposition of retailers, with a broad range of high-quality own-brands, is simplification of choice. In effect, the consumer is sub-contracting to the retailer on non-critical purchase decisions. Loyalty schemes are reinforcing this trend. Where such schemes offer high value rewards and demonstrably better services, consumers will reduce the number of brand decisions made. Consumers are increasingly asked to ally with supply chain partners (see Fig. 2.2). Proliferation in the choice of airline carrier now has a cost associated with it, such as free travel and access to executive lounges.

Mass customization is another factor. It is now possible for companies to organize themselves to tailor their products for individual customers.

Dell computer sells hundreds of thousands of computers each year, each one custom built to individual specification. Dell customers pick from a range of basic chassis and then specify their requirements for hard disk capacity, memory, chip speed, software and connectivity. Within 2 to 5 days their machine arrives at the door. Dell does not keep finished goods inventory in stock. As new technology arrives, it does not incur finished goods write-offs or have its sales people foisting yesterday's technology on its valued clients.

Levi Strauss, makers of Levi jeans, introduced a service whereby individuals' measurements are fed into the production system and jeans are made customized to customers' shapes. Take this on a few stages. We predict that in the very near future, quality clothing retailers will keep highly accurate, virtual dummies of each customer on file. Customers will make an appointment with a clothes consultant employed by the shop to sit down in front of a screen and the virtual dummy in order to create a wardrobe together. Customers will be able to explore a wide range of outfits and assess how these will look on them. The final purchase will be the result of an interactive consulting process that considers colors, cost, time, and style. The reduction in finished goods inventory, end of season mark-downs and unproductive selling time would reduce costs through the supply chain. With appropriate guarantees of customer satisfaction with the finished goods, would not many people sacrifice the choice and mayhem of the modern shopping mall? In such a retailer world, would choice add as much value as it does now?

Customer driven, not cross-selling

As these types of relationships are built with customers, companies add value to their offer by being increasingly driven by customer needs. Progressive business and consumer marketers are trying to position their brand as "supply partner of choice" to the most profitable customers. To compete in this hotly contested arena, brand custodians will have to be able to listen actively to customers and make solutions available at a mutually agreeable price. Customer value is created by directing the entire efforts of an organization and its networks of alliance partners and suppliers toward that aim.

In trying to augment a brand's core functionality, many marketers did little else than try to cross-sell unconnected products while posing as a solutions provider. The failure of the consumer banks to reposition their brands in the 1980s as one-stop financial supermarkets are testimony to the difficulty traditional brand marketers will face when trying to become customer driven.

New competition, financial deregulation, and globalization in the 1980s drove banks to a fundamental shift in their business strategy and hence desired brand positioning. Banks' traditional services were perhaps low-margin and low-growth segments of the market: transaction processing and loans. They felt that they could leverage their customer database, brand strength, and distribution network to sell pensions, insurance and long-term savings instruments. A cry went up through marketing circles suggesting that banks abandon their traditional focus on share of assets to concentrate on share of purse. Banks tried to reposition themselves as financial partners to wealthy individuals.

Regulations have greatly restricted the ability of US financial institutions to offer comprehensive one-stop shopping, but these regulations are being relaxed. In anticipation of a much freer and more competitive market, leading players are considering major acquisitions that fill out their product portfolio and distribution channels. At the time of writing, the Citicorp-Travelers merger was announced; it was the largest corporate merger of all time.

Many European financial markets are much further along the path to deregulation than the USA, and US banks could benefit from the hard lessons learned on the other side of the Atlantic. The initial British experience with one-stop shopping, or the financial supermarket as many called it, seems to have been a failure. The banks appointed customer service managers that did not have the power to make the bank work even for targetted high-net-worth customers. Instead, they appeared to the market as sales representatives for a series of branded products, none of which was necessarily best of breed in its individual segment of the market. The key decisions about rates of returns, terms and conditions were not negotiable: each financial instrument was managed as a stand-alone profit center whose policies were decided by a product-focused marketing team and not a customer-focused one. In the absence of a supplier that is truly customer driven, many customers simply bought the best priced instrument in each of the financial markets from different suppliers.

Jim Patience, Vice President of CSC Consulting and Systems Integration, claims:

> The one-stop shopping strategies of the 1980s failed because they were predicated by the banks' desire to fill their branch networks with new

revenue. The customer strategies of the 1990s abandoned the notion that branch networks must be saved. Instead, modern marketing strategies start with the mission of adding value to specific customers.

Cross-selling, one-stop shopping cannot substitute for a truly customer-driven organization. In the absence of value added, people will buy on price and conditions. Most product brands are not structured to be sufficiently flexible to create this value.

Financial services mergers will not pay back if they are treated as mere product portfolio fillers and channel builders. The emerging organizations must fundamentally change their processes, structures and rewards to create customer-centered businesses that add more value than customers obtain with their existing suppliers.

BUSINESS INTEGRATION

As products become more sophisticated and customer demands on performance and service grow, few companies, if any, find that they can offer the total solution to customer problems. Traditional brand management seeks to wrap the solution around layers of services to provide customers with an integrated and whole brand experience. This tends to create complexity and cost, rather than value. Marketing creates value in the modern economy by integrating the companies' suppliers and manufacturing processes to create value-adding business systems. The structure of alliances and processes needed to create the total customer experience are beyond the ability of traditional product brand management.

As products become more sophisticated and customer demands ... grow, few companies, if any, find that they can offer the total solution to customer problems

IBM is a good case in point. It was the leading exponent of solution selling during the 1960s and 1970s and its methods were widely copied by companies such as Xerox. It created an organization brand based on its product line and augmented with layers of added value services and systems support. The oft-quoted expression that, "You never get fired for choosing IBM" describes a positioning around being the IT manager's supporter and a USP based upon certainty and predictability. The infrastructure needed to deliver that promise proved unequal to the challenge of client server architecture where leaner competitors unbundled IBM's offer and created real or *de facto* alliances that delivered more powerful solutions at lower prices and with better service. Consider Novell, the 1980s start-up that took the local area computer network (LAN) market from IBM in a few short years. Operating through a vast network of Novell-trained third-party distributors, it proved much more agile and competitive than the total solution brand.

Some airline carriers appear to be following IBM down the total solution route but they have learned to implement the total brand experience with third-party partners. The cutting edge of airline service includes picking up and delivering passengers from their homes, loyalty schemes, knowing the reading and eating habits of individual customers, travel arrangements and so on – all in the name of creating the augmented brand experience. To avoid overloading themselves with complexity, BA creates its total brand experience by augmenting its own resources with outsourcers and third parties. AirMiles runs its loyalty program, alliance carriers agree to match BA's quality standards and third-party engineering firms will take more responsibility for maintenance leaving BA to concentrate on customer care and brand development.

Traditional product branding no longer adds sufficient customer value because it is generally a standardized offer which is the result of a functional management hierarchy not structured to be sufficiently broad enough, or responsive enough, to satisfy modern customer demands. Customer value is increasingly generated by business processes traditionally outside the brief of brand management. Those to whom businesses have entrusted their brands are generally operating within a model that fails to address the gap between customer and brand value. Marketing leaders must accept the need for new models of differentiating their organization's offer or they will find themselves increasingly irrelevant to their customers and to their peers.

> *Marketing leaders must accept the need for new models of differentiating their organization's offer or they will find themselves increasingly irrelevant to their customers and to their peers*

SUMMARY

The brand became the centerpiece of many companies' marketplace strategy because it created customer value by mitigating customers' purchase risk: the risk that the product or service would not perform, and the risk that the product or service would say the "wrong" things about the buyer to his/her peer group. The customer value in the brand was contained within the information and reassurance that it provided, thus simplifying the purchase decision through the offer of a unique and recognizable choice.

While it could be argued that brands have existed for over 100 years, it is only in the past 30 that a coherent brand theory has been developed. The cornerstones of this theory lay in three ideas:

- the augmented brand
- the unique selling proposition (USP)
- the 4Ps of product, price, promotion and place.

The augmented brand, illustrated through concentric circles emanating from a core product or service, encouraged managers to wrap their apparently undifferentiated products and services in ever increasing layers of emotional ties and added value services. This ensured an integrated response to the customer's need for emotional reassurance around the product's performance. The USP focused that brand architecture around a concise statement of its long-term, customer-relevant differentiator. It ensured that the integrated response to customer needs was distinguished from those of its competitors. The 4Ps helped the organization to align all its marketing and sales activities around a coherent set of priorities in support of that distinguishing USP. Together, these tools ensured that companies focused their efforts on the creation of products and services that would garner loyal customers bought into the overall brand concept. Customers gave their allegiance to the brands that they selected.

To manage this set of tools and ensure their effective integration, companies adopted the product brand management structure pioneered in the consumer goods industry. Decision making in the organization was delegated to individual product and service champions; the brand became a virtual organization within the overall organization.

We maintain that the link between brand and customer value is often severed. Customers, both in consumer and industrial markets, are finding other means of managing risk than through the purchase of brands. The customer is looking more at the value of the purchase, than the down-side risk. Replacing risk as a prime purchase motivation are some of the key components of value today, namely:

- information and not sales pitches

- relationships with suppliers for a stream of value over time and not a series of individual transactions
- customization to meet individual needs as opposed to a plethora of offerings (choice)
- integrated solutions to individual needs and not just products.

The traditional brand toolset and its brand management structure seem incapable of delivering the modern definition of customer value.

Further reading

Some of the best reading about the power of the brand is to be found in the works of two American authors, David Aaker and Ted Levitt. The leading British writers on the subject include Mark Uncles, Peter Doyle, Leslie de Chernatony and Malcolm McDonald, and books about branding published by Interbrand Plc are to be recommended.

Some of the best critiques of the traditional brand and marketing management have been written by Martin Christopher and McKinsey & Co.

- David Aaker, *Managing Brand Equity*, Free Press, New York, 1991.
- Ted Levitt, *The Marketing Imagination*, Free Press, New York, 1986.
- Leslie de Chernatony and Malcolm McDonald, *Creating Powerful Brands*, Butterworth-Heinemann, Oxford, 1992.
- McKinsey and Company, *Marketer's Metamorphosis*, London, 1994.
- Philip Kotler, *Marketing Management: Analysis, Planning Implementation and Control*, Prentice Hall, New Jersey, 1967.
- Martin Christopher, "From Brand Values to Customer Value," *Journal of Marketing Practice*, vol. 2, no. 1, pp. 55–66, 1995.

BRIDGING THE VALUE GAP

INTRODUCTION

Creating a unique selling proposition (USP) for product brands and exploiting them through predictable stimulus-response tools falls short of the modern customer's level of sophistication. Customer value creation is not captured by the traditional activities associated with brand building, that is the USP, the augmented brand, and the 4Ps of product, price, promotion and place. Today's marketing challenge is to bridge the widening gap between brand and customer value, which is increasingly generated through supply chain leadership, networks of relationships, and individualized customer service. In other words, customer value is created through the alignment of the organization's core business processes to the marketing strategy described by the organization's marketing mix.

UOVP – UNIQUE ORGANISATION VALUE PROPOSITION™

We suggest a concept termed UOVP – Unique Organisation Value Proposition™ – as the modeling tool which marketers can use to bridge the gap to customer value. The UOVP integrates a company's core business processes into a visible set of credentials that add value through the supply chain. The best metaphor for the visible UOVP is that of a cable that envelops, holds, and directs individual wires, each representing a core business process that potentially adds customer value (see Fig. 3.1).

The "brand" to be built is the UOVP, the cable which binds the wires together. It replaces the 4Ps as the primary brand building device as the marketing mix moves from being exclusively product centered to incorporate the means by which the organization creates customer value. Whereas variables in 4Ps marketing remain product–sales related, the UOVP variables are more appropriate to an environment where customer value is created through the activities of the entire organization. These higher level marketing mix variables are the organization's reputation, the performance of its products and services, its product brands and customer portfolios and the network of relationships that it has developed. The product brand is not dropped; it remains a vital part of a broader and more complex structure of customer value.

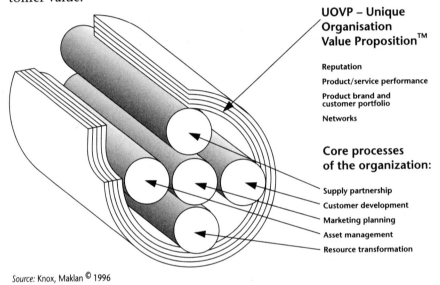

UOVP – Unique
Organisation
Value Proposition™

Reputation

Product/service performance

Product brand and
customer portfolio

Networks

**Core processes
of the organization:**

Supply partnership

Customer development

Marketing planning

Asset management

Resource transformation

Source: Knox, Maklan © 1996

Fig. 3.1 Bridging the value gap

The UOVP is conceived as a means of expressing value in an environment where customer value is inextricably linked to the core processes of the organization that operate end to end serving customer needs. We contrast this with the 4Ps which were developed to communicate value in an environment dominated by businesses where value was created by moving sequentially from product design, manufacturing, selling, and servicing. In the modern, process-led organization, value is created by these activities occurring in parallel and with direct customer involvement throughout. The UOVP marketing mix components are now explained in more detail.

COMPONENTS OF THE UOVP

Reputation

To build a strong reputation, the brand must convey the organization's capabilities and commitments. In a relationship, customers do not want to know only about today's features, they want to know how this relationship will be in a few years' time and that suppliers can maintain commitments over time. Reputation, therefore, cannot be product specific, it cuts across the complete portfolio of the organization's activities and values.

> We, as brand owners, need to build relationships with our consumers, to create a dialogue, expose them to our corporate values; establish a bond based on something more deep-seated then mere product quality, brand image or even simply meeting consumer needs.
>
> *Robert Bailey, Marketing Director, Heinz UK*

The activities that deliver reputation are those that describe the organization's commitments, such as mission statements, values, and ethics. The marketing activities that support this include stakeholder management and internal communications.

Body Shop is an extreme example of an organization that does not talk about its products in any meaningful way – it only refers to its commitments and ethics. The customer is not buying traditional beauty care at Body Shop but rather is engaging in a relationship based on a certain value set. To a lesser extent, Virgin sells its character more than its individual products. Marketing in these organizations is more stakeholder management than classic 4Ps marketing.

The UOVP dimension of reputation differs from traditional corporate positioning as it is based upon the entire firm's capabilities and commitments as opposed to its desired marketplace position. Companies whose performance is inextricably linked to their product portfolio find it difficult to move out of their traditional positioning, even when their capabilities justify it. For example, Xerox has tried unsuccessfully to expand upon its reputation as a paper copier company for decades, and yet its Palo Alto Research Centre (PARC) is widely acknowledged as the inventor of many of the most important personal computing technologies including the personal computer, local area networks, graphical user interfaces, and the mouse. Xerox has simply failed to exploit these inventions successfully on a commercial basis. While there are, no doubt, organizational and cultural reasons behind this, one of its greatest obstacles was that its reputation remained limited to its existing positioning and products portfolio.

Parallels with Xerox exist in other industries. The European divisions of Ford and General Motors have never been able to move from their reputation for "everyday" cars, while Toyota successfully entered the prestige market at its first attempt. Ford's reputation was limited to its product portfolio, whereas Toyota was known for its commitment to quality manufacturing and customer satisfaction: in the UK, its top of the range Lexus is often sold in the same showroom as popularly priced small family cars. According to Lexus, over 90 percent of their customers are aware that they are buying a Toyota. GM and Ford had to buy Saab and Jaguar respectively to enter the high-priced car market. They are still playing the game of managing product portfolios while Toyota builds a corporate reputation based upon a commitment to quality.

Many large and sophisticated product brand owners are communicating corporate values alongside traditional product brands

Even consumer goods manufacturers, the creators of the augmented product brand, struggle with the need to establish a corporate persona that can co-exist with its stand-alone product brands. Traditionally, it has taken the view that customer relationships will be held with product brands and that consumers would not have a direct rela-tionship with the holding company. Some of the largest and most sophisticated product brand owners have moved away from this pol-icy over the past five years in order to communicate corporate values alongside traditional product communications. Nestlé has started to put its brand name on all its products and Lever Brothers in Europe has begun the same process. The balance between product and cor-porate branding appears to be moving more toward the latter among information companies. We would argue that Microsoft is much more the brand than any of its individual products and that much the same could be said of Intel, IBM, Compaq and Dell. If the consumer goods industry was just establishing itself today, would it be so biased toward stand-alone product brands?

UK food retailers have successfully branded their commitment to the customer and built a reputation as the consumer's supply chain partner. Their own brand is a strong guarantee of their efforts on behalf of their customers to provide good value, innovative products, and a convenient, quality shopping experience. When we began our marketing careers, it was the commonly held view that retailers' own-labels could never extend past the basic household necessities. A senior cosmetics marketer once said that consumers will not buy beauty products from the same brand that supplies toilet bowl cleaner. History has proved this wrong. Over the past 15 to 20 years grocery retailers have invested in better retail environ-

If the consumer goods industry were just establishing itself today, it would favor corporate brand identities as opposed to separate product brand names

ments, value added services, employee training, consumer help lines, supply chain efficiency and socially responsible behavior. During this period, the market share of own-label brands has grown to just under 40 percent of the market (see Fig. 3.2). Over the same period food and toiletries brand owners have made unprecedented investments in

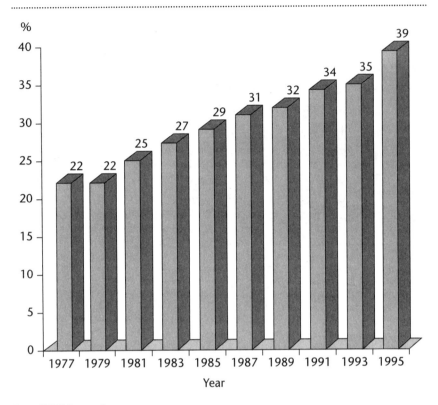

Source: TNAGB Superpanel

Fig. 3.2 UK own-label market share growth, 1977–95

brand advertising, image, packaging, and line extensions. Which has created more customer value?

We maintain that such reputation is best built at the level of the organization. The key elements that comprise one's reputation among customers result from the organization's commitments, its values, ethics, policies and practices. Neither the company's individual product brands, nor its brand managers, have the authority or scope to commit the entire organization in these areas nor to manage the full range of stakeholder relationships necessary to create reputation. Product brand companies build corporate reputation only as a by-product of the marketing efforts behind individual brands.

Product and service performance

Product and service performance delivers the functional performance commensurate with the organization's reputation through its products and services. The capabilities that support performance are product (service) design, manufacturing and delivery. The key marketing activities supporting those capabilities are benchmarking and customization.

In traditional consumer goods companies, brand managers are taught to believe that their brand's functional performance must deliver the expectations created by the brand's promise. That attitude reflects a sequential view of brand building: awareness, interest, trial and repeat purchase. The assumption is that the brand's USP will interest consumers and promote trial. The product, in use, must then not disappoint in order for trial to evolve into some degree of brand loyalty. In today's markets, we maintain that brand loyalty is not an automatic follow-on from interest and trial.

Faced with apparent declines in brand loyalty, one observes that brand marketers are coming around to the view that having a product that merely satisfies customers' expectations is no longer enough – one must *delight* the customer. However, what remains to be proved is whether or not the customer wants a large number of suppliers to delight him or her. For many categories of purchase, the customer merely wants competence. For example, how many opportunities do manufacturers of branded aluminum foil have to delight their customers? Telecom experts suggest that residential subscribers contact their supplier every seven years, usually when they move house. How many opportunities are there to really delight their customers? Perhaps the customer merely wants a guaranteed 24-hour, year-round dial tone at a good price. Exhortations to delight customers are well intentioned, but we believe that

> *Brand loyalty is not an automatic follow-on from interest and trial*

many brands facing declining shares cannot delight their way to improving their relationship with the customer.

The problem, we suggest, is that simply managing the traditional 4Ps definition of performance is no longer enough to deliver sufficient levels of customer value in the most competitive markets. The manner in which Tesco has overtaken Sainsbury's in the battle for market leadership in the highly sophisticated UK grocery market illustrates this point. Arguably, Sainsbury's is the equal of Tesco in all the 4Ps: price, product quality and range, promotion and place. Yet Tesco's performance, as seen by the consumer, is stronger. Tesco has concentrated on aspects of performance measures beyond the 4Ps, such as regularly being first to introduce new value added services including loyalty cards, financial services and guaranteed short queues at the cashier. As a consequence, it has developed a reputation as the more progressive grocer of the two and is using this to create more powerful relationships with the most profitable consumer segments. Determining the measures of performance upon which customers will evaluate the firm is one of the strategic roles of UOVP design.

There is also a more traditional aspect to performance in UOVP brand management, that of design to build functionality at a competitive price. Mercedes is another example of a very powerful brand, dominant in its market sector, which failed to align its performance measures with those that create value in the modern economy. Its business suffered in the early nineties, particularly in the USA where the brand lost a lot of its following to Toyota's Lexus. We can assume, for purposes of this discussion, that their cars were always of excellent design, build and performance; they probably succeeded in delighting the customer. The Mercedes brand is one of the world's most powerful: it is universally known as a symbol of prestige, luxury, and exclusivity. However, it was clear at this time that brand value, and the performance its cars delivered, were not generating as much customer value as its competitors. The price Mercedes expected consumers to pay for its product was no longer commensurate with competitive offers in the same sector.

Helmut Werner, then CEO of Mercedes-Benz, recognized that his cars were overengineered and began to address the problem. He is quoted in an industry magazine at the time outlining a change in direction for Mercedes. His intention was to change the company from being a producer of luxury cars only to an exclusive, full-line manufacturer offering high quality vehicles in all segments. Mercedes was forced to look beyond the traditional 4Ps brand management. The traditional definition of "premium" positioning was not working.

The Mercedes C class was an early product of the new policy. Priced and engineered to be more competitive in the executive saloon market, it was both popular and a contributor to the automaker's image. In 1997, Mercedes launched the A class, a small car for the European market. Its small size and low price point represented breakthroughs for the company while the car's revolutionary design generated excellent reviews from the pundits. Unfortunately, Mercedes had to halt production of its new car shortly after launch due to the possibility of it tipping over under extreme maneuvering conditions: the Swedish moose test. Other car companies have suffered highly public recalls in the past and Mercedes is confident that the new car will prove to be a success when it is relaunched on the market. We are convinced that Mercedes' new product and pricing strategy will guarantee its future prosperity. Mercedes today is certainly not repositioning itself away from its reputation for premium quality. It is now using a broader definition of performance for premium quality to close the gap between its brand and customer value.

Product brand and customer portfolio

Organizations also manage a portfolio of product brands and customers in addition to their overall reputation and performance. Many times these portfolios are at odds with each other, leading to customer confusion and organizational disunity. The UOVP, with its richer mix of variables, offers companies a way to align the management of different identities within the organization and its customer groups.

One of the most challenging marketing issues in many organizations is managing the relationship between the corporate brand and its product or business unit brands. The discipline of the USP, with its narrow encapsulation of customer value, often creates irreconcilable differences between individual operating business units or product brands and the owners of the corporate identity.

Companies that have adopted variations of the brand management structure plan their activities on the basis of the portfolio of products and services they sell. Each product line, or line of service, is managed as a business that must justify itself on the basis of net present value (NPV). If a brand's projected cashflows, discounted by an appropriate risk adjusted rate of return, are positive, then the brand is retained in the portfolio. If negative, the company has one of three choices:

- improve the cashflows
- reduce the investment
- remove the brand from the portfolio.

Dividing the organization into a series of discrete product brand groups, each measured by NPV or a proxy thereof, is an effective means of managing complexity. However, as we have discussed earlier, managing brand portfolios does not always address the modern generators of customer value.

Increasingly, the marketplace demands that we manage a set of relationships with customers and not just a portfolio of products and services. Companies are shifting their marketing focus from product to customer. A customer-based equivalent management tool to the product NPV is the estimated lifetime value of each customer across the organization's brand portfolio. Customer-led marketing departments segment their markets and plan activities on the basis of NPV measures of each customer group, not brand group. Traditional 4Ps marketing does not strongly embrace such customer segmentation and management due to its focus on product. The marketing tasks for the management customer groups are database management, loyalty management and effective discrimination of offers between customers. These tasks are hard to integrate into an organization divided into product brand groups, each with its own relationship with the customer.

Brand and customer portfolio management create value in different ways. Brand portfolios allow companies to transplant their knowhow in different situations. McDonald's or Burger King can set up an outlet at a highway service area and instantly attract customers. Customer value is created because each customer knows exactly what he or she is buying even in an unfamiliar setting. 7-Eleven can brand the gasoline companies' forecourt food stores in much the same way. The product portfolio of these UOVPs are easily understood and highly transferable. They create value through their information content. However, the product brand is only a *component* of the UOVP, a *portion* of the customer value creation, and *not* the object of it.

Customer portfolio management also creates value and, increasingly, marketing pundits observe that customer portfolio management is more profitable than product portfolio management. In Garth Hallberg's book, *Not All Consumers are Created Equal*, extensive research demonstrates that even for mass consumer brands, often less than 20 percent of the households contribute the vast majority of profits. Conversely, brands actually lose money when sold to as many as one-third of their current customers. This is a further substantiation of the 20/80 rule that business-to-business marketers have known to be true for decades. If only 20 percent of the addressable customers are worth serving, a firm that has built relationships with high-potential customers manages a valuable asset which should be communicated to its suppliers and potential partners along the value chain.

Some companies overtly brand their customer portfolio. SABRE and SITA, the international travel and banking IT services companies respectively represent customer-based propositions. SABRE was developed and launched by a major international airline carrier with the dual purpose of providing the backbone of its reservations systems and establishing a new industry standard that favored its solution. It is now being opened up so as to be less proprietary. The power of SABRE lies in the commitment of its biggest customers. Similarly, SITA was a telecom service provider owned by the world's major banks to provide interbank settlements. It is now being commercialized and is selling its services to third parties. Its proposition, at least initially, was largely based on its experience and knowhow forged through its relationships with the banks.

Many large and complex organizations, particularly suppliers of information technology products, have found that the best way to manage the constant flow of product innovation was to organize along world product markets. Moto-

There remains a strong need for a corporate essence that transcends individual product ranges

rola has integrated world management structures for its mobile phones, pagers, computers, smart cards and chip product ranges. Hewlett-Packard has world strategies for PCs, enterprise computers, medical equipment and scientific testing equipment. There is probably no other practical way of keeping ahead of the new products and technologies in these fast-paced businesses. Nonetheless, many organizations of this type find that there remains a strong need for a corporate essence that transcends individual product ranges and have created integrating structures so that certain stakeholders can relate to the business as a whole. For instance, as home use of technology expands, companies such as

Motorola will find that they are increasingly in the consumer electronics business so they are making provisions which allow major
electrical retailers and consumers to access the company irrespective
of the individual product bought.

The UOVP creates a brand presence that allows companies to hold
relationships with key stakeholders, both as a series of product brands
and as an integrated company. It is one means of resolving the inher-
ent trade-off between the transaction or selling focus of the USP and
the interactive and less predictable nature of building relationships
with individual customers. Management of the UOVP creates a
process that strikes the balance between managing product portfolios
and customer relationships in order to add the most customer value
for each company. Most important, by managing this component of
the UOVP, one ensures that the balance is created at a sufficiently
senior level in the company to ensure that the nature of customer
relationships is not a mere by-product of individual product brand
management structures.

Networks

The extent to which your business partners add value to your final
offer, and the level at which this contribution is made visible to the
customer, determines the extent to which an organization brands its
network of relationships. Managing a brand which depends on the
contributions of others is one of the most difficult challenges facing
companies today. However, many companies now find that their network of relationships provides their best differentiation to competition. The narrow focus of the USP and 4Ps marketing make it difficult
for marketers to fully incorporate the potential added value of
alliances in their brand offers. The UOVP makes this value added
through networks an explicit part of the customer proposition.

It is increasingly common for companies to form highly visible alliances in order to service customers. Traditional alliances were often driven by the economic logic of reducing cost or excess capacity in a particular industry. In the 1990s we have witnessed imaginative combinations of capabilities from separate companies operating in different industries which create new bundles of customer value. In the USA, AT&T offered a novel combination of phone and credit card with VISA to quickly become one of the largest credit card issuers. JP Morgan, one of the world's largest investment bankers, outsourced information and communications services worth $300 million a year to a consortium led by Computer Sciences Corporation, which included its rival Andersen Consulting, AT&T and Bell Atlantic. This consortium won the contract against the world's largest IT services supplier, EDS, which bid as a single company.

These bundles are different from mere supply chain partnerships where a company outsources the production of key components but still badges the final offer with its own name. In the examples we have just examined, the customer is made aware of the various component suppliers because the seller believes that the visible alliance of the brands created a more powerful proposition.

In addition to these examples of co-branding, some companies overtly brand their network of relationships. Part of their proposition is that when you "buy" them, you get access to a large number of value added partners.

One of the ways in which Computer Sciences Corporation distinguishes itself from companies such as IBM, Andersen Consulting and EDS is through the quality of the faculty engaged in its research programs. Through the company's research center, CSC actively engages the insight and the intellect of some of the world's most prominent technology and management thinkers such as Alan Kay, Nick Negroponte, Philip Kotler and Charles Handy. This virtual network creates one of the consulting world's most important think tanks and provides customers with a high level of creativity and future orientation to the solutions offered by CSC. Its network of thought leaders features prominently in CSC's brand proposition.

Consumer loyalty reward schemes are a further example of branding one's network of relationships. Like many airlines, British Airways created a stand-alone brand, AirMiles, to anchor a vast network of famous brand names associated with travel. This creates value by allowing customers to collect points towards free air travel through this network. Smart Card, a scheme started by Shell, took this logic one step further in Scotland where it announced that customers have the opportunity to spend loyalty points with any of its participants.

Electronic communities represent another means of branding one's network. CompuServe, the on-line services giant, offers its subscribers access to discussion groups with its other members. Computer enthusiasts find that they can post a question to the appropriate discussion forum and have an answer back from another member within a few hours. For CompuServe, a large proportion of its brand's value added proposition is the network of customers posting messages.

THE UOVP MIX

The mix between the components of the UOVP creates the organization brand and the means by which the organization brand is differentiated from its competitors. Company brands that rely on the creation of a USP often find that the traditional branding tools are too narrow and focused to capture the totality of a company's value adding capacity. This is particularly true for large, diverse, and mature companies that participate in a number of markets and at different levels of the value chain. Conversely, broad corporate statements designed to be inclusive are often seen as "motherhood" or irrelevant and many fail to distinguish the company. UOVP branding allows for clear and distinguishing statements to be developed for each of the four elements, and is therefore inherently broader and more customizable than the traditional USP of product branding.

The credit card business provides examples of companies that have well-conceived brands that communicate more about the corporations than their products (Table 3.1).

American Express is relentless in its determination to keep hold of the market's big spending executive travelers. Its value proposition

Table 3.1 UOVP mix for credit cards

	American Express	MasterCard	Discover
Reputation	Successful people Elite, well off Club Global Travelers' product	Ubiquitous US brand	Fit-for-purpose Middle class Low cost, few frills US brand
Product and service performance	Globally effective Unlimited credit One high standard of customer service Reliable Trouble with merchant acceptance	Fit-for-purpose Service varies by issuing bank Accepted everywhere (in USA)	National level of service High standards of service Low costs Questions on acceptance
Product brand and customer portfolio	Strong brand and co-branded portfolio Upmarket user group High spend per user Not always used as everyday card	Expanding product range No distinctive consumer segment Often the base card for usage	Limited product range (now expanding) Often a second card
Networks	Originally stand-alone limited network Increasingly travel-related co-branding	Tie with retail banks Penetrating into every usage opportunity (i.e. government, grocers) Globalizing the brand	Original tie to Sears Limited co-branding

rests upon a globally consistent, high-quality service particularly suited to its core customers who require unlimited credit on demand, extremely well-presented billing information and global reach. It has had to expand its product portfolio to compete with the no fee and co-branded cards; however, business partnerships are well thought through in terms of impact on brand image and mutual profitability. Another strand to the strategy is to increase the at-home usage and not as a mere traveling aid. It is improving relationships with merchants and adding new services that encourage greater usage (for example, booking theater tickets). At its most aggressive, it is mounting a legal challenge to the VISA and MasterCard dominance of retail bank issuing. For American Express, universal recognition and service delivery to its target audience are key to its success. It is successfully balancing the four UOVP variables to remain true to its reputation, while meeting competitive attacks on performance, portfolio and networks. The challenge in managing the American Express UOVP is achieving the right mix that does not jeopardize the exclusive nature of the brand.

Discover is one of a number of 1980s new entries into this market. Backed by Sears, it grew quickly to become one of the largest card issuers in America. Its offer was low-cost, fit for purpose credit cards for "middle-America." Few of its users require the global functionality of American Express and wish to pay for it. This is not a new marketing proposition and we can find similar strategies in telecommunications, airlines, hotels and retail markets. The challenge in managing its UOVP is to maintain a real cost advantage while not falling too far behind on product performance, portfolio of products or networks of relationships. Discover must continually review what is the right balance between cost and benefit for its target market.

MasterCard is far more ubiquitous, perhaps through its long association with retail banks. More people have access to the card, charges are lower than AMEX (but higher than the low-cost entrants) and almost all merchants accept them. It lacks the prestige value of the

AMEX card and the global brand name that appeals to international travelers. It added functionality to its products and created a gold card to increase its appeal to the biggest spending customers. It has also acted aggressively to globalize its brand to appeal to international travelers. MasterCard was reported to be ready to spend £100 million (approximately $160 million) in order to buy back its UK brand name of almost 30 years (Access) from its issuing bank partners. The figure was never confirmed, but in 1997, Access became MasterCard. On the Continent, Eurocard is being de-emphasized wherever possible in favor of the US brand name. MasterCard occupies a great middle ground between the functionality of specialists such as American Express and fit-for-purpose challengers. Its mix of reputation, performance, services and networks seeks to borrow from each of its competitors in order to minimize share erosion. MasterCard will fight from the middle ground by segmenting its customer base so that it remains competitive for individual customers while maintaining its ubiquitous, all-occasion, reputation.

UOVP AND CORE PROCESSES

When the company's core processes are driven by the UOVP brand, the UOVP moves deep into the organization and creates a proposition that is not only relevant to customers but is sustainable over time.

Most organizations in the west have recast their activities from being driven by discrete business functions to end-to-end, cross-functional, value adding processes. The core processes which deliver value to customers will vary by industry and by company within industry. While we do not presume to suggest a "general theory" of generic processes and process management, we believe that the UOVP will work across most process designs. For the purposes of this book, and based on our consulting experience, we develop the UOVP on the basis of the five core processes shown in Fig. 3.1:

1 **Supply partnership** – The ways in which an organization develops its "inputs" from suppliers for the production of its goods and services.

2 **Asset management** – The way in which assets may be developed to add value to those inputs. Assets include knowhow, people, product brands, patents, as well as plant and machinery.

3 **Resource transformation** – The way in which assets are deployed against inputs to create goods and services for sale to the next level of the value chain.

4 **Customer development** – The process which addresses the balance between customer acquisition and retention from a detailed knowledge of customer motivation, purchasing styles and purchasing strategy. Customer development also involves building the relationships with the preferred customer groups identified through this strategic analysis.

5 **Marketing planning** – The activities that develop and sustain the UOVP brand which are very different from conventional product-branding practices. Managing the UOVP marketing mix means driving the organization's brand values through the end-to-end business processes that deliver customer value. This can be achieved by marketing planning that supports both the development of this UOVP marketing mix and priorities across core processes.

Marketing planning stands apart from the other four core processes in that it is internally focussed, although it may involve benchmarking both customer and supplier perceptions of value. The marketing planning process that supports the UOVP is discussed in the next chapter since we believe it is essential for effective development of the organization brand.

SUMMARY

While we are not alone in arguing that brand marketing is in transition, there seems little in the way of a systematic framework for taking it forward. This makes it difficult for business leaders to redirect their efforts to those activities that generate customer loyalty and preference for the organization's goods and services.

The problem facing many companies is that they are directing substantial marketing investments with an old toolset that was created for a past business climate. Companies cannot create sufficient levels of customer value by pulling upon the traditional levers of the 4Ps.

The modern environment requires a new conceptual framework and toolset. We propose UOVP – Unique Organisation Value Proposition™ – that replaces the USP and 4Ps as the primary focus and toolset for value creation. The metaphor for the UOVP is a cable and wires. The wires are the core business processes that add value through the supply chain to the customer while the cable houses and directs these processes end to end. The cable is the brand, the entity which the customer touches and sees, but underneath it lies the processes that are delivering the value.

The UOVP builds a branded proposition that is based upon the levers that are relevant to customers today, namely: reputation, performance, customer and product brand portfolios, and networks. These levers are best managed, indeed in some cases only manageable, at the level of the enterprise and not the product line. Therefore, the focus of branding will move to the organization.

Just as a cable is not very useful without wires, the new levers of value creation are only sustainable in the marketplace when they align the company's core business processes to the UOVP brand proposition. The UOVP therefore becomes a tool both of differentiation and of process integration for the company.

Further reading

Readings around this chapter could encompass all that relates to creating customer value in the modern economy. Hammer and Champy's book *Reengineering the Corporation* is probably the most famous book in this area, and it describes the ability of business processes to recreate customer value. Both authors have followed up with separate books on the same subject.

- Michael Hammer and James Champy, *Reengineering the Corporation*, Harper Business, New York, 1993.

Jan Carlzon, former CEO of SAS wrote a famous book on leadership that is worth reading just for the opening comment that "we used to fly aeroplanes and now we fly people." Jan Carlzon is associated with the concept of moments of truth, the millions of contacts between people and customers and the need for the entire organization to live its values each time. This gives us some indication of how pervasive the brand needs to be through the organization to be effective.

- Jan Carlzon, *Moments of Truth*, Ballinger, Cambridge, MA, 1987.

We would also recommend the Treacy and Wiersema book for its description of the need to align the company's value proposition with its internal operating model (business processes) in order to succeed in the hyper-competitive marketplace of today.

- Michael Treacy and Fred Wiersema, *The Discipline of Market Leaders*, Addison-Wesley, Reading, Mass., 1995.
- Garth Hallberg, *Not All Consumers are Created Equal*, John Wiley, New York, 1995.

MARKETING PLANNING

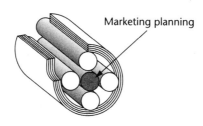

Marketing planning

INTRODUCTION

In our experience, marketing planning has evolved around the creation and management of products and services. The goal of the marketing plan is often to decide the extent to which investments will be made in support of current products and services, in extending the current portfolio into new markets and in developing new products. These decisions are made in consideration of "top-down" objectives or assumptions about the company's financial target and a "bottom-up" estimate of the potential of product and service portfolios to deliver against these targets. Increasingly, companies conduct a similar review between investments among its customer groups in order to match customer plans with product portfolio plans. This approach generally results in a compendium of individual plans, based around the expected market performance of core products, and the budget forecasts of key customers and integrated by a process of negotiation between marketing, sales, finance and, ultimately, the representative of the shareholders.

As the gap between brand and customer value widens, it is no longer sufficient to engage in product and market planning in a "top-down and bottom-up" approach. In much the same way we acknowledge the demise of product branding in earlier chapters, it is important to recognize the limitations of traditional planning that has informed brand decision making and the implementation of marketing programs. These limitations are addressed in the early part of this chapter.

The new role of marketing planning is to provide a broader route map which enables the UOVP architecture to be formulated for the purposes of directing the organization's core processes. In this chapter, we consider the shift from what we term the traditional planning process to that which we propose to support UOVP architecture. We do not tackle the wider strategic planning agenda of defining the organization's core competencies and processes. Instead, we discuss planning in the context of the core processes that have become the most widely recognized. Although they cannot be regarded as universals, we see the process of marketing planning itself as being critical in all companies for the reasons presented later in the chapter.

The question we wish to tackle, therefore, is why this shift in the marketing planning process from being incremental and product centered to being cross-functional and value centered is necessary.

LIMITATIONS OF THE TRADITIONAL MARKETING PLANNING PROCESS

In most organizations, marketing planning is an annual process that reviews the external environment (market place, customers, competitors), identifies the gaps between that environment and the company's current portfolio of goods and services and creates an activity plan to close that gap. Sophisticated companies employ a number of planning tools in this process. Most readers will have some experience in using a number of them – SWOT Analysis (Strength Weakness Opportunity Threat), customer research, Gap Analysis, Boston Consulting Group Matrix, Ansoff Matrix and the Directional Policy Matrix.

Generally, it is the product and/or brand management team that champions the process, given the custodial nature of their job and their knowledge of competitive activities and market structures. In some instances, account plans are also drawn up by key account management to ensure that the strategies of their most important customers are reflected in the planning process. Where there is a high degree of integration between the sales and marketing functions, a combined customer/brand plan emerges which serves to provide a checks and balance system in implementing customer marketing and product-brand marketing activities (see Fig. 4.1).

The two dimensional nature of this system and the level of integration which it represents, illustrates perfectly a number of underlying shortcomings of traditional planning.

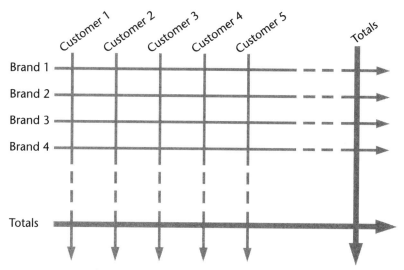

Fig. 4.1 Marketing planning matrix

Planning is productcentric

The tools of marketing planning assume that we can determine distinct markets based upon products and services and that the object of planning is to determine the optimal product portfolio. Hamel and Prahalad, in their famous management book *Competing for the Future,* illustrate the shortcomings of limiting strategic thinking in such product-constrained silos. They might claim that planning should identify the "white space," the large and unexploited chunks of new customer value, as a more worthwhile objective. The plan should go beyond product and customer activities to identify and develop the organization's core competencies needed to exploit the identified white space.

We endorse this point of view fully. In our experience, breakthroughs in marketing rarely come from planned activities around the current product and customer portfolios. The breakthroughs which all managers wish to emulate, such as Walkman, Post-It, CNN and much of the information technology now sold, did not arise from a gap analysis grounded in the current definitions of product, markets and customers. It is now almost legend that IBM did not initially believe that "the customer" would want a personal computer. In many ways, companies' marketing imagination is constrained by the product–market silos in which they believe they compete.

> *In many ways, companies' marketing imagination is constrained by the product–market silos in which they believe they compete*

Planning is incremental

Generally, next year's volume is based upon a combination of this year's sales to customers and the historical growth (or decline) in product sales against a forecast market share projection. The future is considered to be an extension of the past. Discontinuous change is very difficult to incorporate into traditional portfolio-based processes.

IBM and Digital likely suffered from incremental planning and failed to fully understand how the move to desktop computing would transform their marketplace and customer demands. Their costly infrastructure, based upon solution sales and service, was undermined by low-cost, flexible computers supported by more open technical architectures.

In the early 1980s, Xerox's planning was based upon individual product lines and ranges but failed to account for Japanese competitors undermining the entire business model by using third-party distribution for smaller copiers. Xerox was forced to rethink its entire proposition and reengineer most of its business processes to respond.

Planning is sequential

Although consultation across other functional domains is sought, the company marketing plan essentially reflects 4Ps marketing: price increases, distribution targets, product relaunch timings, and promotional activities on an account basis. The planning process is from left

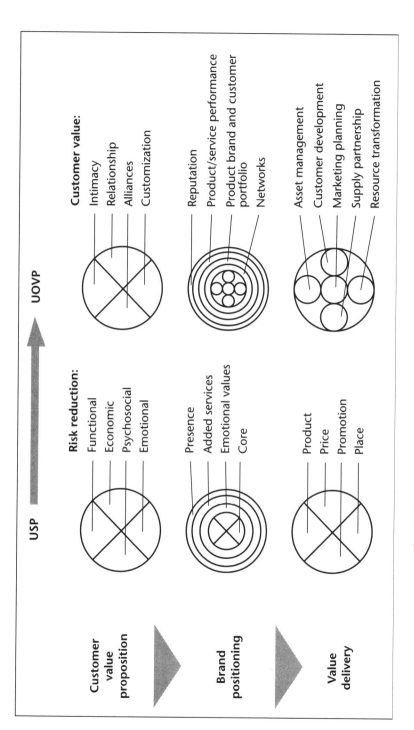

Fig. 4.2 From product-centric to process-based planning

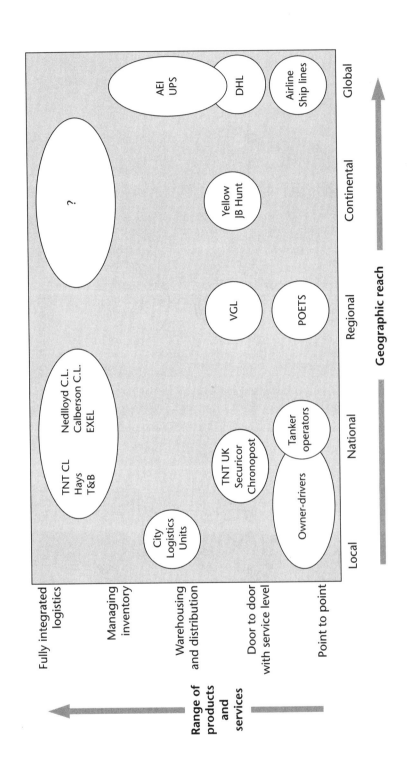

Fig. 4.3 Current competitive positions in logistics supply

Source: Adapted from IBM Consulting Group

The worldwide logistics director for a global computer company in the USA summarizes the direction in which customer value drivers are developing:

> Six years ago we had 35 significant logistics vendors, we have now reduced this to about five. International product flow should be within the capability of anyone, information flow is when competitive advantage can be achieved.

The physical activities have largely been relinquished by such multinational customers, but as vendor consolidation initiatives are introduced, process integration skills and information flows become critical and rate determining in the levels of added value activities that can be outsourced in their end-to-end supply chain. The drive toward increasing process content, away from physical delivery, marks the evolution in thinking about what creates customer value in this industry (see Fig. 4.4).

The challenge to suppliers will be to determine their levels of participation in this emergent environment. Those with a mission to become integrated logistics suppliers will need to reevaluate their business objectives as customer value is redefined in these terms.

Currently, there is a value gap between customers' future needs and the performance of individual logistics companies. No one company can come close to delivering the necessary skills and capabilities at the high added value levels and few can offer a product and service portfolio that meet their more immediate needs outside the confines of national or regional boundaries.

The drive toward increasing process content, away from physical delivery, marks the evolution in thinking about what creates customer value in integrated logistics

Continuing with this integrated logistics example, the next question for each supplier becomes, "Where are we now and what vision of value do we have for the future?" The current levels of value delivery are relatively straightforward to audit by competitively bench-

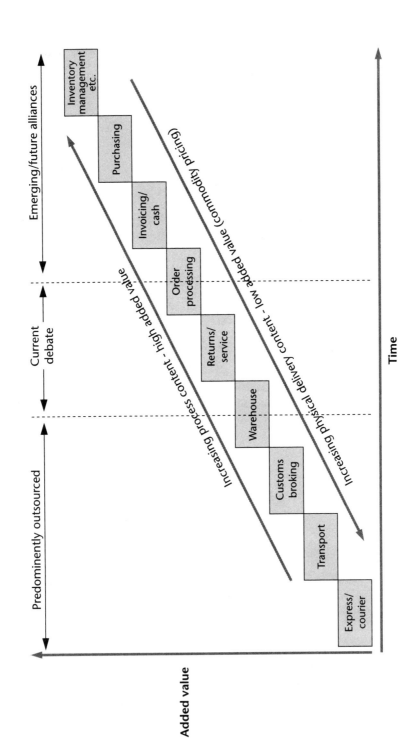

Fig. 4.4 Creating customer value in integrated logistics

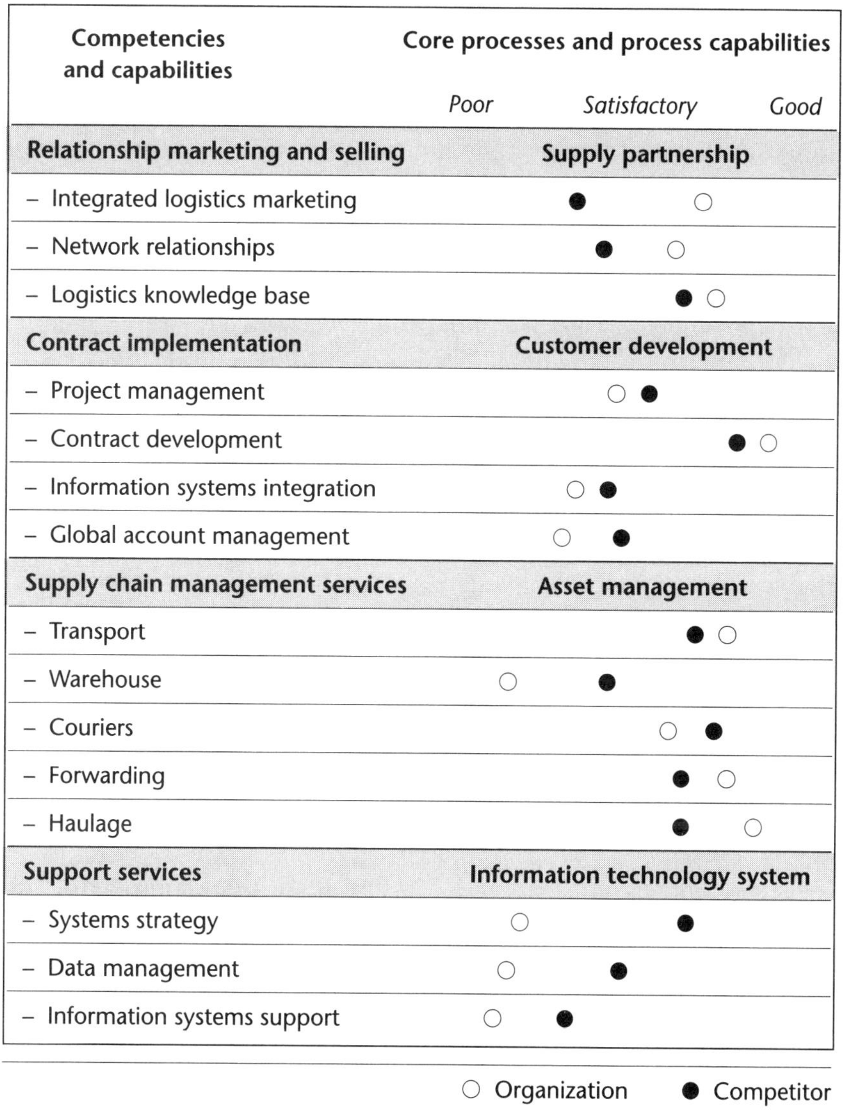

Competencies and capabilities	Core processes and process capabilities		
	Poor	Satisfactory	Good
Relationship marketing and selling — **Supply partnership**			
– Integrated logistics marketing	●	○	
– Network relationships	●	○	
– Logistics knowledge base		●	○
Contract implementation — **Customer development**			
– Project management		○ ●	
– Contract development			● ○
– Information systems integration		○ ●	
– Global account management		○ ●	
Supply chain management services — **Asset management**			
– Transport		●	○
– Warehouse	○	●	
– Couriers		○ ●	
– Forwarding		●	○
– Haulage		●	○
Support services — **Information technology system**			
– Systems strategy	○	●	
– Data management	○	●	
– Information systems support	○	●	

○ Organization   ● Competitor

Fig. 4.5 Benchmarking core processes

marking their core processes against the performance of other organizations within the sector. An example of such a benchmark is set out in Fig. 4.5.

Set against the customer's perceptions of future value requirements in integrated logistics is the gap between the organization's current activities and how it would wish to create value as a logistics provider. This analysis will lead directly to business objectives aimed at closing down the gap. It may be that the organization's "vision of future value" or its business aims may not fully coincide with the value gap perceived by customers in this particular example. The domain of UOVP architecture and planning is, therefore, to define a route map between the organization's mission statement and value delivery through its core processes and networks.

Planning the UOVP brand positioning

UOVP brand positioning is the result of creating the appropriate mix of reputation, performance, portfolio and networks that distinguishes the company's customer value offer from those of its competitors. This mix is best designed at the organization level for it is only the entire company that can support most of the mix variables. In this way, UOVP planning is different from the traditional productcentric process it replaces.

In identifying the contribution which each element of the organization's marketing mix makes to the customer value proposition, the logistics company just discussed found it necessary to extend the capabilities for which it is known by incorporating strategic alliances. The UOVP architecture and planning provides direction and a system for the development of its emerging network of supply partnerships, alliances and co-branding activities. Importantly, it also focuses attention on product and service portfolios and their performance levels, whether branded by the organization itself or through these alliance partners.

Through this customer value planning, the senior management team recognized that it could not develop all the necessary competencies needed to provide customers with products, services and process integration on a global basis. Nor did it regard this as necessary since flexibility and customization are also customer requisites. However, by selecting key customers and working with them in developing appropriate services in-house and through alliances, an integrated logistics requirement could be met.

The challenge to UOVP management in this example is to fix the boundaries around the products, services and other capabilities which need to be retained and developed within the organization and which are assembled externally through alliances and suppliers. For instance, if the information technology system is weak relative to competition (see Fig. 4.5), a case could be made to partner with companies that can help the company to fully exploit the business benefits from new technology. Where aspects of asset management such as warehousing are also weak, alliances could be built on a regional basis to integrate appropriate warehousing facilities. As the organization wishes to lead the network through its ability to create integrated partnerships capable of meeting individual client needs, a strong reputation for managing IT systems (design and integration) and customer development is both strategic and essential for the desired brand positioning. The company must continue to build their management skills and competencies both internally and externally to support these processes on a global basis.

Inevitably, choices about the ownership of capabilities and processes, and where the internal-external boundary lies, are linked to wider choices about global stretch, brand development, and performance. For instance, in our example key performance indicators throughout the entire integrated supply chain will be needed to monitor deviations from standards agreed with global customers. These can range from customer satisfaction measures with the account team to throughput times and cost to service. The brand portfolio determines the levels at which outsourced activities, alliances and supplier partnerships are connected to the organization and communicated to customers through advertising, promotion and word of mouth. In some instances, co-branding may enhance reputation while, in other situations, outsourced arrangements may be subsumed within the organization's brand name and structure. The reputation of the organization needs to be proactively developed and the building blocks for future reputation management – the competencies and core processes that enhance the organization's reputation – planned systematically.

There is an interdependency between each of the four organization marketing mix elements: who you work with and how you brand the offer combine with the perceived levels of performance to determine what your reputation is. It is by determining what it is you want to be known for among primary customers that your "vision of value" and your organization's positioning in the value chain is determined. Reputation is the enabler for building a strong brand name which itself depends upon consistency in positioning and superior performance in these broader organizational terms. Successful branding and reputation management is likely to lead to more business from existing customers and to attract new customers.

Since imperatives in product and service performance, brand portfolios, and the range of customers served are used to inform the nature of relationships both within the organization and outside its boundaries, the reputation of the organization is either advanced or diminished over time according to how effectively the UOVP is implemented. How this UOVP architecture is conceived and how it is perceived by customers, therefore, has a profound influence upon which of the organization's core processes and network relationships dominate as they are the means by which customer value is delivered.

Who you work with and how you brand the offer combine with the perceived levels of performance to determine what your reputation is

Value delivery planning

As the mechanism for creating customer value extends beyond 4Ps marketing, successful implementation is entirely dependent upon the organization's core business processes being aligned to its brand positioning and working with mutually supportive organizations to provide the customer solutions. The UOVP provides an architecture of brand and process development so that alignment can be achieved internally and with alliance partners.

The UOVP brand positioning sets the scene for process planning and implementation. The cable and wires metaphor developed in Chapter 3 clearly acknowledges this relationship. So, process goals are determined from the UOVP, as are their relative importance in delivering customer value. The fact that there are explicit guidelines and policies which characterize the UOVP marketing mix means that this cable has a visible set of credentials that position the organization in the supply chain. These credentials offer differing things to differing companies in the network of relationships since they are seeking to engage with the organization to achieve differing goals. However, because the organization's credentials are clear and explicit, they effectively bind the wires together and direct them toward particular customer groupings while also enabling alignment with suppliers through partnerships, strategic alliances and outsourcing relationships. Some of these wires or core processes will necessarily be customer facing while others will be directed more toward suppliers and organizational resource transformation.

It could be argued that because it is the quality of the relationships along the processes and in the network that help create customer value, the real purpose of marketing management is to facilitate and manage these relationships. In a highly integrated network, customer and supplier processes are aligned to those in the organization which are critical for achieving successful working relationships along the supply chain (see Fig. 4.6).

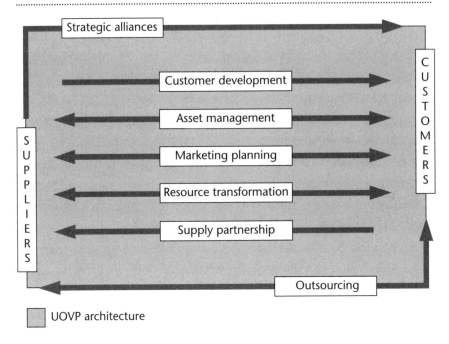

UOVP architecture

Fig. 4.6 Process and network integration

This move toward network integration is being pursued by grocery retailers. At a recent conference in Birmingham, England, Tesco called together its top 400 suppliers to announce an end to the "copycatting" of major brands and to seek new ways of working together with their network of suppliers. In a move that reflects UOVP thinking and UOVP architecture, Tesco's senior management will make store data available to its key brand suppliers. The purpose is to gain insights into consumer purchasing preferences using the marketing expertise of these suppliers. This move toward shared skills and knowledge with retailers, and away from mere product supply and replenishment, means that the customer development teams within brand manufacturers will help shape category pricing, product range and a deeper understanding of portfolio purchasing among target consumers. Tesco is also seeking greater supplier transparency in both suppliers' capacity, costing and raw materials – a development which is viewed by suppliers with some trepidation as the retailer attempts to extend its relationship management networks to raw material suppliers. One supplier referred to this as "my factories are your factories." Viewed from the suppliers' perspective, this initiative by Tesco to develop strategic supply partnerships – category captains – could signal a further intent to move toward co-supply. In this instance, co-supply suggests an ability by category captains to form strategic alliances with branded and own-label competitors to provide category "solutions" for its retailer customer. Any such branding organization which is unfamiliar with such networks will need new skills in network relationship management if it is to create customer value and be "branded" by the retailer as potential channel captaincy material.

In contrast to the co-supply implications of alliances, outsourcing is generally considered to be an arrangement through which processes and capabilities are delivered by a third party. It implies the transfer of company assets and responsibilities to the third party who provides economies of scale and scope and add value through superior knowledge. Both strategic and non-strategic activities may be outsourced, usually because the capability is seen as being outside the organization's core processes. For instance, British Airways has outsourced many ground activities, such as baggage handling and engineering, in order to focus on the customer development process, as competition intensifies and the opportunities for mass customization increase. In the new mission statement, "to be the undisputed leader in world travel," the strategic intention of BA to move away from being "British" and "Airways" to becoming a global provider of travel-related services is clear. In this shift toward a broader range of customized services, advantageous partnerships have been developed with Hertz, Forte hotels, British Telecom, Diner's Club and a number of other airlines. From BA's perspective, these strategic alliances form a branded value network intended to create a "whole customer" approach to travel management for its Executive Club membership.

Some organizations, such as Guinness and Levi's, are making the transformation from product to process planning in support of their UOVP brand positioning. Project Condor was launched by Guinness management in 1994 precisely for these reasons: its objective is to deliver the "Perfect Pint in Every Pub." Guinness had recognized that its performance in bars was not consistent with its brand positioning which could only be implemented through end-to-end delivery of the product to its consumers across both the off-trade and on-trade. In the on-trade, this resulted in the reengineering of the delivery system and channel management through the installation of special founts to aid the famous two-part pour and the training of licensees in storage and how to serve the perfect pint.

Levi's brand positioning is inexorably linked to being a cutting-edge, youth fashion statement. At Levi's, the brand team is committed to the "Staying in Tune" planning program which works across several core business processes to deliver value for its 15–25 year-old target market. From a communications point of view, the brand must stay in tune with current music trends: "If popstars wear our products, then sure as hell consumers will." The knowhow of tying into the right musicians and concerts is a core element of what we would define as asset management.

At the retail level, "In Tune with Now" builds retail partnerships that focus on its target audience rather than just selling jeans. Levi's adopts a three-tier approach to managing these retail relationships in an attempt to match the style of the consumer purchasing process by store type (see Table 4.1). If you accept that the purchase environment is part of the delivery of their product brand values, then this is an example of aligned customer development with the organization brand positioning.

The development of the Original Levi Stores, which are fully owned by the organization, allows for experimentation in store atmospherics and sounds, merchandising and the customization of their tailored jeans. These stores provide the foundations for the product brand's premium status which has been maintained at about 30 percent throughout the 1990s. They also offer an appropriate environment to communicate the company's heritage and reputation through its work in the community with the Levi Strauss Foundation.

Table 4.1 Levi's channel and product portfolio

Consumer purchasing style	Store type	Product portfolio
Opinion leader	Original Levi store	Opinion products
Early and late adopter	Jeans specialist	Seasonal core + basics
Mainstream	Departmental store	Top 20 selling lines

In a sense, both Guinness and Levi's have moved beyond effective process management to build greater customer value by concentrating on the specific needs of distinct customer groups. In the case of Levi's, this is achieved by balancing product and customer portfolios through their retail customer development process. In Guinness it has been achieved by reorganizing around "demand companies" for both the on-trade and off-trade which are supported by a consumer marketing group that optimizes the marketing resources around the "whole" consumer, whether s/he is purchasing Guinness products in

Both Guinness and Levi's have moved beyond effective process management to build greater customer value by concentrating on the specific needs of distinct customer groups

the pub or for home consumption. In both organizations, customer value is created through the supply chain by processes that support the product brands and services delivered at point of sale.

IMPLEMENTATION ISSUES

Both the content and context of marketing planning is radically different in organizations that wish to achieve process integration. By shifting away from a product-focused ritual to addressing the determinants of customer value that create competitive advantage, the marketing planning process becomes inclusive. This is entirely consistent with the move toward flat structure organizations and process-based management. To achieve a greater degree of customer intimacy and customization, through relationship management and network alliances, requires new thinking about the means of achieving business objectives and measuring the risks they represent to the organization. While it is still superior products and services that deliver superior profits, the context in which they are created, purchased and consumed has altered beyond all recognition in many industry sectors.

The challenge to marketing management, if indeed marketing is to lead the development of UOVP architecture, will be to provide the team leadership in redefining planning across the organization. Marketing should clearly play a leading role in scoping the research and competitive analysis which draws together the determinants of customer value during the auditing stages.

Marketing should also play a leading role in the visioning for the future but it is often constrained by its current tools and brand custodianship agenda. However, positioning the organization in the value chain by defining the UOVP architecture – the organization's marketing mix – is a strategic decision that needs consensus throughout the organization and a case could be made for its ultimate ownership in the boardroom. Assessing and directing the organization's reputation, its product ranges and performance criteria, against this background of alliances and networks, provides the strategic framework for the organization's future growth prospects. In essence, these are the credentials of the organization and require concurrence at the highest level. This framework provides the blueprint for subsequent process and network planning.

Ownership issues surrounding process planning are conditioned by whether or not the process is customer facing. Inevitably, all processes have customer implications but those that impact most on customers – those that need to be aligned against customer processes – could well be planned by marketing and sales people as process owners. Setting process goals and determining resource requirements, both in terms of budgets and people, is a further responsibility of the process team. Once formulated and agreed by senior management, the same process teams are responsible for program implementation.

Building and managing the network beyond core processes also needs meticulous planning. Again, predominantly customer-facing relationships, particularly those with co-branding implications, could be led by marketing. If the resource is more supply based or if outsourcing is the key activity being planned, then the lead planning role may be headed by supply chain management or finance.

The prominence of brand and customer planning in this wider process is diminished. Nonetheless, given the importance of the organization's key products and services, 4Ps planning is still necessary. Awareness, affinity, availability and price still drive success in product and service branding. Since product and customer portfolio management form part of the UOVP architecture, this functional planning activity becomes a sub-set of the overall process and network planning.

In structuring this book, we felt it important to engage our readers at an early stage in the planning of this organizational approach to branding. This process is represented as the central wire in our cable and wires metaphor (Fig. 3.1) and we argue throughout this chapter that it is critical in linking both these aspects of the organization together. If it is the cable that binds the wires together and provides strategic direction, it is this planning process that provides the glue of integration and alignment.

In subsequent chapters, we explore other core processes which are considered endemic to the organization to show how best practices can create customer value throughout the entire organization. The additional four core processes selected as being representative of the organization's value adding capabilities can be regarded as neither definitive nor inclusive, as we mentioned earlier. For instance, consumer organizations such as Unilever would choose to separate consumer development from customer development, due to their position as brand manufacturers in the supply chain. Rank Xerox, in business-to-business markets, identify 14 processes that are deemed to be of strategic significance in creating customer value and serve to define the organization's position in the value chain. Whether this number should be deemed five or 14 is really the concern of a wider strategic planning agenda. Our concern, from a branding perspective, is to explore the relationship between the UOVP and the most widely recognized core processes.

In Chapters 5 through 8, we explore this relationship following an input–output approach to the business; that is, the start of the value creation is with the inputs (supply partnership), it continues with the application of the company's assets to those inputs (asset management), transforming the inputs to outputs (resource transformation) and, finally, the outputs find a home with customers (customer development).

SUMMARY

Traditional marketing planning is characterized by a bottom-up compilation of individual product and customer account plans integrated into a top-down demand for sales and profit. The process is typically led by the custodians of the product brands.

It fails to create a series of activities that add sufficient levels of customer value and tends to be productcentric when increasingly this customer value is no longer just about products. The process tends to build targets through incremental achievements based upon the past while the real breakthroughs are to be found in discontinuous change. Traditional planning is sequential from marketing to the other functional groups, whereas value creation comes from an interactive relationship between doing–learning, doing some more, and learning some more. It is often divorced from the day-to-day value delivery to customers and frequently the attendant wishlist of marketing activities is not designed for rapid and efficient implementation.

UOVP planning starts with revisiting the entire notion of customer value in the business and encourages the development of bold, breakthrough new marketing ideas. A brand positioning for the organization is created through the four variables of the UOVP which we believe are more relevant to today's customer than the augmented brand it replaces. Finally, it integrates the core business processes of the organization and its partners to deliver the promised customer value: the business processes deliver far more value than the 4Ps they replace.

Marketers should be well placed to lead UOVP marketing planning because of their intimate knowledge of customers and competitors and their reputation for intuition and creativity. However, the current tools with which they work, and the product–market silos in which they operate, might limit marketing's ability to become the natural UOVP architects within their organization. Marketers need to broaden their understanding of customer value and cross-functional value delivery in order to create UOVPs for their organizations.

Further reading

Most of the classic texts on marketing planning have been developed around product portfolios and customers. While this process is still necessary it now becomes part of a much wider activity of process planning. Malcolm McDonald's text on marketing planning provides a very comprehensive step-by-step guide to product planning.

- Malcolm McDonald, *Marketing Plans – How to prepare them: how to use them*, 3rd edn, Butterworth-Heinemann Ltd, Oxford, 1995.

In his book, *The Rise and Fall of Strategic Planning*, Henry Mintzberg looks at the faultlines in classic planning procedures. Although the context is strategic planning, the learnings can also be attributed to marketing planning in organizations.

- Henry Mintzberg, *The Rise and Fall of Strategic Planning*, Free Press, New York, 1993.

At the time of writing, we are unaware of a specific book or text that develops a methodology for planning along processes. Clearly, Gary Hamel and C.K. Prahalad provide a very comprehensive approach to competency-based planning in their widely read book, *Competing for the Future*. Although competencies and core processes are closely linked, the flow nature of process management distinguishes it at a planning level.

- Gary Hamel and C.K. Prahalad, *Competing for the Future*, Harvard Business School Press, Boston, MA, 1994.

Martin Christopher makes a *cri de coeur* for a systematic approach to process planning in *Marketing Logistics*. The arguments he presents in Chapter 7 are compelling.

- Martin Christopher, *Marketing Logistics*, Butterworth-Heinemann Ltd, Oxford, 1997.

Finally, although not specifically about planning, *Beyond Re-engineering* by Michael Hammer presents a very strong case for process-centered management in the reengineered organization. The case studies he provides look at the competitive advantage benefits that can be derived. It is not, however, a book about process alignment.

- Michael Hammer, *Beyond Re-engineering*, Harper Business, New York, 1996.

SUPPLY PARTNERSHIP

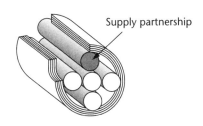

Supply partnership

INTRODUCTION

Branding is as much about integrating suppliers in a value chain as it is about creating awareness and interest among prospective buyers. Today, a successful brand is supported by a powerful network of suppliers that enables it to deliver its promise to customers. Supply chain management is no longer purely an operational matter considered the domain of logistics and purchasing departments. It is a strategic program necessary for the organization to achieve its quality, cost, flexibility and innovation missions. The UOVP can help organizations manage and add value throughout the supply chain. Perhaps even more importantly, we suggest that establishing supply strategy in the absence of an UOVP architecture may limit a company's ability to add value commensurate with that delivered by competitors.

> **Branding is as much about integrating suppliers in a value chain as it is about creating awareness and interest among prospective buyers**

TRADITIONAL SUPPLY PARTNERSHIP

Traditionally, the management of suppliers was divorced from the process by which marketers sought to create value for customers. Knowing the customer and the market were the primary tasks of the marketing department, or those fulfilling that role. Once marketing determined customer needs, it would work with engineering to decide upon a design that customers would want at a price that customers were willing to pay. Manufacturing would pick up the engineering design and develop a long list of individual components for purchasing to source. Purchasers would be tasked with achieving the lowest cost procurement to the fixed specification. The strategies of supply chain management included:

- multiple sourcing to get prices down and ensure back-up supply
- standardization of engineering specifications to permit more suppliers to bid
- determination of purchase quantities to optimize between component and inventory holding costs.

Decomposing the product brand into minute components focused supply chain management on cost, and not sufficiently on value, quality and innovation. As a result, companies in highly competitive markets found that they were too slow to bring out new products, quality failed to meet customers' expectation, and, despite the focus on component cost, the total cost of manufacture and support was too high.

The problem, we maintain, with traditional supplier management, was that it divorced supply from the creation of customer value. The UOVP seeks to reintegrate suppliers into customer value creation by redefining the role of marketing from "owning the customer" toward the creation of business systems; the integration of core processes into a customer value proposition. To illustrate how this works in practice, we discuss the automotive and UK grocery industries where supply partnerships are changing the buying companies' customer offer, value proposition and competitive strategy.

THE CHANGING NATURE OF AUTOMOTIVE SUPPLY PARTNERSHIP

The automotive industry in crisis

From a position of unassailable strength in the 1950s and 1960s, the US car makers faced serious competition by the late 1970s. Japanese competitors had seriously eroded the market share of traditional brand leaders and at one point, their combined US market share approached 30 percent. There was one year in the 1980s when the bestselling car in America was the Honda Accord.

The existing business model of the American car makers looked unsustainable. Car makers' resources seemed to be more focused on creating brand image, style and emotional appeal than upon engineering, quality and reliability. The marketing strategy of General Motors, the Mount Olympus of the industry, was based upon maintaining its competitive advantage of scale in manufacturing, distribution and advertising. Critical to that strategy was a product brand portfolio approach that created lifestyle selling propositions for each of the Cadillac, Buick, Oldsmobile, Chevrolet and Pontiac marques. General Motors did not appear to have a well-articulated customer proposition around performance, quality, value, ethics and customer service. Consumer activism, US-style litigation and loss of market share to better built small Japanese cars began to make quality, design and time-to-market for new cars, serious commercial issues for GM and the other American makers.

The two OPEC-inspired oil crises of the 1970s further exposed the vulnerability of American car makers. Their portfolio of large, energy inefficient models needed to be updated. For some automakers, their first attempt at smaller cars exposed the inflexibility and sluggishness of their product development process. It was widely reported in the management press that it took Japanese companies such as Honda only three years to develop a new car while it took most western-based companies at least six. A recent article in the *Harvard Business Review* suggested that, throughout the 1980s, Chrysler Corporation's 5500 engineers and technicians could develop only four new vehicles.

The downsizing of cars also brought into sharper focus a large western cost disadvantage to the Japanese despite the economies of scale enjoyed by the Americans. Moreover, many consumers were not willing to pay that premium in order to drive "American iron." Some consumers decided to break the habit of a lifetime and buy "foreign."

Despite public protestations of unfair competition, one suspects that the US car makers realized that their organizations could have been more efficient and competitive.

For some, it was a struggle merely to survive: Chrysler Corporation was rescued by the American government; Ford and General Motors posted some of the biggest corporate losses ever made by a US public company. Likewise in Europe, British Leyland lurched from crisis to crisis, as did many of the state-subsidized European manufacturers.

Better customer value from the supply chain

Manufacturers were forced to look for entirely new methods by which they could take large elements of cost out of each car while improving product quality and reducing the time to develop new models. The automakers had to do more for less, and they had to do it more quickly. "Business as usual" was not an option in this environment and automakers began a process of experimentation to create more value that continues today.

Part of the early programs involved harder negotiations with suppliers. One such initiative from General Motors was merely to announce that it was cutting all suppliers' prices: take it or leave it. Such "hard" negotiating tactics made the entire supply chain take the problem of cost competitiveness seriously. In practice, it served only to push costs down the supply chain to small component suppliers. Some suppliers, particularly those that were not unionized, could take cost out of the supply chain by reducing real wages and benefits but, by and large, "hard" negotiations did not eliminate the large elements of cost that the industry needed to find. The large manufacturers could force margin reduction on the supply chain only to a certain point; somewhere the costs had to be paid.

The next stage for manufacturers was to eliminate time and cost from the entire supply chain: the starting point of this effort was sharing information about production and new product development. One such example was Chrysler, a company that used to devote 12 to 18 months in its new product development process just to send out bids and negotiate with suppliers. This time and excess inventory added cost to car development and production without generating any commensurate value to the customer. By extending the production and planning processes to include suppliers, this could be vastly improved upon and inventories throughout the supply chain could be sharply reduced. Cooperation on new product development allowed suppliers to compete on the basis of adding value and innovation as well as speed up the entire process.

Case histories reported in management literature suggest that such programs took some $400 to $500 off the unit cost of a car. Equally, cooperation with suppliers took months, if not years out of the new product development cycle. If one assumes that a model's marketing life is fixed, the value of each month of selling a new model ahead of competitors is likely to be enormous. We do not know of any car makers that have not undertaken such programs, nor any that do not claim to have generated important savings in time and money.

Simultaneously with these time and cost reduction programs, manufacturers instituted quality improvement programs, some under the banner of total quality management (TQM) and quality circles. The drive for quality, coupled with JIT manufacturing, also necessitated a completely different relationship between supplier and manufacturer. The days of inspection and rejection were finished. Final car quality could not be better than the quality levels achieved by suppliers, so manufacturers began sharing their quality knowhow and training with their suppliers. Industry experts suggest that the more progressive companies are now extending this service to their suppliers' suppliers, realizing that this is where the next wave of gains is to be made.

In the automotive industry, these suppliers are increasingly being asked to take responsibility for complete systems such as braking, drive train, interior, steering and engines, and not just specified components. This allows car manufacturers to derive maximum benefit from suppliers' greater knowledge in each of their areas of specialization. As one industry expert said, "Where do you think ABS braking systems came from? The car makers or the suppliers?"

The relationships between levels of the supply chain have come 180° from where they were 15 years ago. The imperative to improve quality, reduce costs and introduce new products faster forced car makers to abandon the sequential approach to car design: that is marketing judging consumer tastes through engineering, purchasing and the specification of components to be sourced cheaply. Companies no longer maintain that they have the breadth and depth of skill, nor the strategic need to keep the product design and specification in-house. Automotive brands are no longer built by marketers who "know" the consumer and advertisers who know how to communicate and create emotional appeal. Strategic partnerships for sub-assemblies have created a situation where key suppliers generate an increasing portion of the brand's customer value proposition and contribute strongly to its future designs.

Suppliers take more responsibility for value creation

The trend toward suppliers generating an increasing proportion of the final value of automobile is, we believe, set to continue for two reasons: fully integrated manufacturers cannot keep competitive across all the technologies, nor can they afford to continue dealing with many suppliers.

Manufacturers cannot hope to keep pace with developments across increasingly sophisticated technology. Allan Hughes, Sales Director for Motorola's semi-conductor business in the UK, claims that cars can now contain 100 micro-controllers. It is not possible for automotive engineers to read the development of micro-controllers, a product that looks at technology lifecycles in months. Looking to the future, one can make similar assumptions about the new technologies of nano-engineering, "smart" materials, and mobile data management. Product development partnerships are ever more important as automotive technology becomes increasingly complex.

Nor can manufacturers provide the necessary management resources, time and energy to partner with the thousands of suppliers with whom they traditionally dealt. The anecdote about Chrysler spending as much as 18 months just to process paperwork for component bids is evidence to this fact. Inevitably, the more sophisticated a company's approach to supply partnerships, the sharper is the reduction in the number of direct suppliers to the manufacturer. Those no longer dealing with the manufacturer become sub-contractors to the remaining strategic partners. Most, if not all, automakers have dramatically reduced the number of suppliers with whom they deal, allowing the remaining suppliers deeper partnerships with them. We are aware that Rover had almost 2000 suppliers about ten years ago, but expects to have only 200 by the year 2000. The press has reported that Volvo's newest multi-use car chassis models will require only 150 suppliers. No doubt that readers from within this industry will be able to provide anecdotes that trump even these achievements.

> *Product development partnerships are ever more important as automotive technology becomes increasingly complex*

Car makers will develop new value creation roles

One important implication of the increasing contribution of suppliers in the automotive industry has been the internationalization of quality. Some branded car makers will admit, privately, that there is little to differentiate between cars of similar price brands in terms of performance, quality and reliability. We predict therefore, that margins from "bashing metal" will decline and car makers will increasingly look to profit from the services around personal transportation.

As global, effective supply chains enable more companies to create world-class products, the successful branded automaker of the future will have developed strong skills as a business system designer and automotive systems integrator. The bulk of the value added sub-assembly design and manufacturing will be the provenance of strategic suppliers. Brand owners will provide supply chain leadership and integration around a much bigger promise than that offered merely by their cars' functionality. This will accelerate what we propose is the trend away from unique selling propositions, based upon product brands, toward the development of Unique Organisation Value Propositions which are based upon a much broader range of personal mobility commitments that are most credibly offered at the level of the organization.

This point is illustrated in Fig. 5.1 which suggests how the implicit UOVPs of today's car makers could evolve. The traditional UOVP is dominated by the car makers' product portfolios, product performance and after-sales support. The core business processes needed to support this are resource transformation (manufacturing) and asset management.

As world-class suppliers drive out poor quality and unnecessary costs from the marketplace, car maker UOVPs can support broader propositions than product alone. In Fig. 5.1 the future UOVP is likely to be more balanced and supporting a wider reputation and a visible network of alliance partners than is the case now. Customer development and the building of supply partnerships become the most important business processes in this scenario. However, it is no accident that in this future scenario, the business process wires in Fig. 5.1 are generally wider than our assessment of the current situation

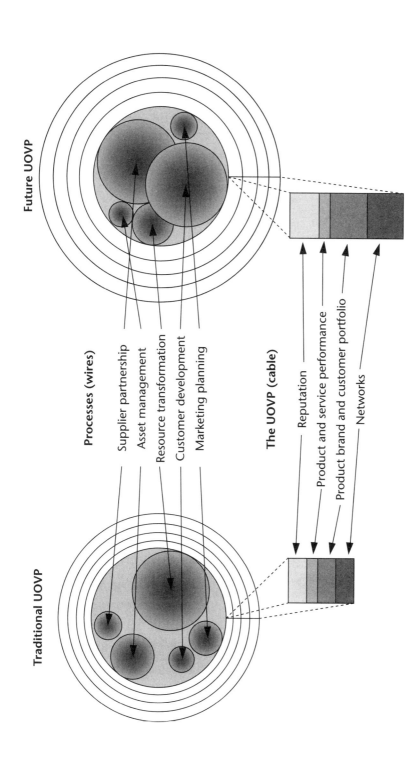

Future UOVP

Traditional UOVP

Processes (wires)

Supplier partnership
Asset management
Resource transformation
Customer development
Marketing planning

The UOVP (cable)

Reputation
Product and service performance
Product brand and customer portfolio
Networks

Fig. 5.1 Changing UOVP architecture

would suggest. Car makers will need a broader base of skills and competencies if a more balanced UOVP is to be realized.

One can already observe that car makers are bundling ongoing service, repair, insurance, reselling and personal finance into their branded offer. General Motors has successfully entered the credit card market in the USA. Looking further ahead, we predict that mobile, online data capabilities will be added to cars over the next decade. According to press reports automakers are trying to establish proprietary information systems to dominate the information around driving. Services emanating from this may include navigation, preventative maintenance, fleet management and security.

This scenario, if indeed valid, has important implications upon the traditional role of marketing as arbiter of consumers' needs (tastes), value designer, and starting point of the product development process. Increasingly, it is the supplier base that creates new consumer benefits through its understanding of evolving technology and its affordability. New services will be introduced with much support from strong business partners that know more about consumer demands within the new service area than marketers working in the automotive industry. Automotive marketers can therefore no longer design consumer value in-house; marketing leaders should be creating alliances that provide their brands with better supply chains and more innovative new services.

Traditional, USP-based marketing, with its strong emphasis upon creating brand differentiation around the product, its core functionality and its emotional appeal, did not prove sufficiently broad to meet the Japanese threat. The most successful responses to competition involved creating broader, organizational value propositions delivered by significant improvements in supply partnership. It is interesting to ask if the architects of such value creation came from marketing departments or from purchasing, manufacturing and logistics?

FOOD RETAILING

UK food retailing provides an example of a value chain that, unlike car making, did not start from a position of vertical integration. The industry is now dominated by branded leaders of strong, virtually integrated supply chains that compete for customer business. In the UK, each supply chain is led by one of the multiple retailer brands such as Tesco, Sainsbury's, Asda, Marks & Spencer (M&S), or Safeway. These brands dominate consumer relationships and occupy the commanding heights of the supply chain. They supply a significant proportion of their consumers' total food and related item spend with products bearing their own names, yet do not possess a single factory between them. Their suppliers enable them to create customer value in excess of that created by their competitors.

A tradition of low value added

With the growth of competing chain stores, UK food retailers faced ruinous price wars in the 1970s and early 1980s. At that time, they competed by selling cheaply standardized manufacturers' national brands in a bid to maximize store traffic and, they hoped, the spend generated by that traffic. The retailer brand was generally "undervalued" and based upon basic attributes of location, selection, hygiene, and price.

In North America, food retailers invested in better stores, added value services and better business processes in an attempt to compete on a higher value added basis and with higher margins. Where American supermarket chains developed own-brands, they often positioned them as low-priced propositions; the Ontario-based retailer, Loblaw, was the notable exception to this policy. Relationships with customers were based on special offers, location and store appearance. In some areas, deep-discount prices were advertised weekly and smart consumers made separate lists as to what to buy in each grocery chain in order to take advantage of the "hottest" weekly offers. Retailers educated their customers into low-priced buying strategies. Statistics published by Procter & Gamble confirm that the average American visits supermarkets more than twice weekly, suggesting that consumers partition their purchases to take advantage of the best deals.

British food companies have adopted a different policy. While appearing to imitate the USA in developing new outlets and business processes, to a much larger extent they have developed high-quality own-label products, valued organization brands and stronger relationships with consumers. They have created supply partnerships that allow them to exploit new markets and compete with advertised brands on both price and quality, while beating them on flexibility and innovation.

Initially, as with the car industry, the food retailers used their supply chains to remain cost competitive. Over time, they appreciated that their own products represented a valuable brand and competitive weapon. Perhaps it was the example of Marks & Spencer Food Halls, or learning from the experience of Loblaw in Ontario or the intensity of the national rivalry between Tesco and Sainsbury's, but the sophisticated retailers determined that all items carrying their brand logo would support a strong organization proposition.

As quality and own-label based competition advanced, retailers encouraged their suppliers to produce better tasting and more innovative products than competitors' suppliers could. These policies, over time, have created powerful retail brands in which consumers invest tremendous faith.

> *Sophisticated retailers determined that all items carrying their brand logo would support a strong organization proposition*

Marks & Spencer provides an excellent case in point. Its policies over time have created a corporate image of quality, value and trust. Survey after survey demonstrates the high regard in which the British public holds the company. Its food products are perceived as more innovative with higher quality and taste attributes, worthy of a premium price. A colleague recently reported a conversation he had with one of its competitors, wherein the competitor complained, "When we are out of stock on an item, the customer is irate with us for our failure. When M&S is out of stock, the customer is mad at herself for not getting there earlier."

Yet the M&S proposition is delivered by its network of suppliers, a fact which is not at all hidden from the public. Its well-known supply partnership program enables the company to extend its influence from the raw material suppliers through the production of finished packaged foods. It often works with suppliers that are of a size to be strongly influenced by Marks & Spencer and ultimately become its only customer. M&S's supply chain management is based on long-established personal networks, total supplier commitment to M&S, and shared interest. The company has created a customized, but virtual supply chain. It sells only the products of this supply chain. M&S competes as a complete supply chain against other supply chains much more than as a retail product against the Tesco and Sainsbury's "products."

Food retailers in America do not enjoy a similar degree of control over the supply chain. In fact, powerful national brands still enjoy the dominant role in such categories as soup (Campbell), diapers (Pampers) and even aluminum foil (Reynolds). Nonetheless, even the owners of the most dominant brands are under relentless pressure from retailers to become better business partners. P&G may be leading the way through its Every Day Low Pricing strategy and much has been said about the supply chain partnership between Wal-Mart and P&G. This is in sharp contrast to the equally well-publicized conflict between the same Wal-Mart and Rubbermaid. Looking at these two cases, it should not surprise us that most of the major consumer goods manufacturers are well advanced in change programs that create partnerships with retailers. Strong brands are necessary for that relationship to work, but manufacturers accept that they must be seen to be contributing to retailers' goals. The goal for the manufacturers is not only to keep marketing directly to consumers, but also to establish themselves as preferred partners to the retailers. This policy will secure retail support for brand promotion, new product introduction, line extensions and logistics, and as a strategy is often termed "category captaincy."

Value creation in the future

As the major companies develop equally competent supply chains, we suggest that the next wave of competition will be in the bundling of diverse household products and services under the management of the retailer. In the UK, retailers have successfully entered the gasoline business and a few of the financial services markets. Tesco has launched a range of baby products through its loyalty schemes. We are aware that the major retailers are discussing distribution of gas and electricity with privatized utilities. The press has reported that Asda, another grocer chain, will distribute British Gas.

In these new markets, retailers have partnered with established brands to provide them with the capabilities that they lacked. We maintain that without the availability of high-quality supply partners, UK retailers would not be able to compete successfully, for example, in financial services markets. In the retail business, the leading edge of supply chain strategy is to buy in capability and not just tins of baked beans.

In the retail business, the leading edge of supply chain strategy is to buy in capability and not just tins of baked beans

Suppliers enable their customers, the retailers, to expand their relationships with the end customer and not just fulfill agreed specifications for commodity food products. They enable their retailer customers to create broadly based Unique Organisation Value Propositions that extend far beyond the value added offered by traditional selling propositions.

A TREND TOWARD HIGHER LEVELS OF SUPPLY PARTNERSHIP

These automotive and retail examples can be seen as part of a trend for suppliers to contribute ever-greater proportions of the final customer value proposition of the brand.

The partnership continuum

We propose that there is a partnership continuum for suppliers which can be divided into four discrete levels, as shown in Fig. 5.2.

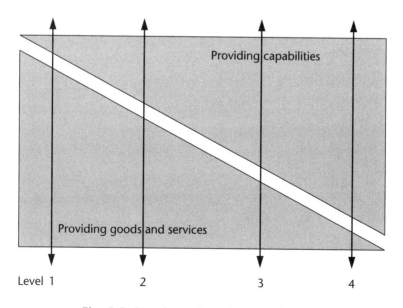

Fig. 5.2 Supply partnership continuum

At each level of partnership, the supplier provides both goods and services, as well as its capabilities. However, the mix becomes more weighted toward the supplier's capabilities with higher levels of partnerships.

Level 1

Traditional supplier that has a transactional relationship with the brand owner. The supplier sells specified goods and services to the brand owner on the basis of price, service, and quality. In most instances, the supplier adds limited value to the brand and is not explicitly part of the brand's customer proposition. This is the traditional buyer–seller relationship.

Level 2

Supply chain optimizer that works in cooperation with the brand owner to reduce total cost (increase total benefit) of the brand's customer value proposition. The supplier is a key part of the brand's ability to compete cost effectively and a valued member of the brand owner's team. However, it is rare for the supplier to be an explicit portion of the brand's customer proposition. Procter & Gamble's work with food retailers on everyday low pricing is an example of supply chain optimization as is JIT and kanban systems in the automotive industry.

Level 3

Supply chain partner that takes responsibility for a significant proportion of the brand's value delivery. Partners not only optimize the supply chain, they take some responsibility for innovation in their area of expertise. Suppliers in this area can contribute a large portion of the brand's value to customers and at times become an overt part of the brand communications. Strategic sub-assembly deals in the automotive industry characterize this level of supply partnership. The contributions that category captains make to food retailers is a further example of Level 3.

Level 4

Value chain partner that enables the brand to extend past its traditional competencies. For example, the Bank of Scotland is a value chain partner for Sainsbury's, allowing it to extend credibly into financial services. We predict that value chain partners, more so than suppliers operating at lower levels of supply partnership, will become an overt part of the final customer offer. In the USA, for example, Federal Express delivery will become part of Internet-based shopping brands' total customer offer. Automotive component suppliers may be badged in-car in addition to the automaker; this already happens with tires and stereos. We believe that Level 4 partnership is not necessarily the same as component branding such as Aspartame, Gortex or VISA. Component brand owners can trade at lower levels, but can also exist at Level 4. Level 4 partnerships exist because of a strategic decision to access a broad range of new competencies.

With the most sophisticated companies encouraging higher level supply partnerships, we are witnessing the creation of an ever-more effective third party supply resource that contributes an increasing proportion of the brand's customer value proposition. In most instances, this resource is independent of the brand owner and high-level suppliers' competencies are available to the brand's competitors. As these suppliers generate increasing proportions of customer value, those value areas will become less effective brand discriminators. The brand owner will be forced to develop new areas of value creation in order to prosper.

> *The brand owner will be forced to develop new areas of value creation in order to survive*

Impact of higher level partnerships upon automotive branding

We have already made the point that automotive and retailing industries are moving toward an increasing number of Level 4 partnerships. We can make some assumptions as to the evolution of supply partnerships in those industries and the impact upon branding.

In the automotive industry, suppliers are taking an increasing responsibility for the development of their customers' new car models. Over time, the major automakers will be de-skilled in some critical areas of design and manufacturing and become dependent on efficient third parties for these capabilities. The role of the automaker in such a scenario will be that of developing and managing a supply chain that delivers effective business systems and integrating the suppliers' skills into an effective automotive product range. The current automotive brands will develop and integrate new business systems for after-sales services and product lifecycle management in order to differentiate their brands from increasingly similar products. Car makers will move from being "metal bashers" to business systems designers and integrators. Much of the value added component design and manufacturing will occur with suppliers and the industry will create virtual supply chains that compete with each other; much like the present structure of the UK food retailing industry.

We see some evidence of this in the trend for automotive brands to bundle under their own brands third-party car recovery, car loans, car insurance, used car sales and credit cards. Some automakers are taking bold steps to increase their management over their dealer networks in Europe in order to better develop their customer relationships through the product lifecycle and into their secondary lifecycles. Dealers regularly pick up and deliver customers' cars for servicing, provide free loaner vehicles, and use databases to post timely service reminders. Further ahead, "smart" cars with mobile data connections to service centers will alert drivers to poor automotive performance and suggest preemptive maintenance. The same technology will allow faster recovery and better roadside services should that be needed. Car makers or their dealers will use information about individual driving patterns to help specify subsequent car purchases and optimize the performance of the customer's current car. Flexible supply chains will allow a much greater ability to customize the actual performance of cars around personal driving needs and styles.

During the writing of this book, we overheard a dealer service manager admonishing one of his service clerks for not understanding customer priorities when taking a call from a customer with a broken car. "The customer isn't interested in getting his car fixed, he is interested in remaining mobile," lectured the manager. The car purchase of the future will become more of a medium-term contract for personal mobility than a one-off purchase of metal. The brand, the Unique Organisation Value Proposition, will represent the organization's ability to manage this contract, this relationship, with the customer over the complete lifecycle of the product. The automotive marketing department will take on the tasks currently associated with business-to-business supplier management. Brand building will add to its current product-centered focus a relationship and customization focus. This will be facilitated through automotive brand owners' increasing use of Level 4 partnerships to provide the capabilities needed to create differentiated, personal mobility propositions.

One other prediction based upon this scenario: as the traditional automakers move from creating brands around their products, they will increasingly see the benefit in allowing their Level 4 suppliers to brand components that provide immediate reassurance and quality signals to customers. We call this the "Intel Inside" approach. Level 4 partners that could merit the right to co-brand might include those in Table 5.1.

Table 5.1 Co-branding partners of the future

Brand	Component or competency
Motorola	Mobile telecommunications and data
Pilkington	Glass
Chubb	High-security locking and alarm systems
Lucas, Perkins	Engines
IKEA	Interiors

In this scenario, Level 4 partners that prosper will have developed into household brand names. Automotive suppliers are currently concentrating upon the rationalization of suppliers as predicted under Level 3 partnerships. We suggest that as the supply chain strategy evolves, supplier partners will add value to their offering by becoming well known for a limited set of capabilities among their customers' customers.

Impact of higher level partnerships upon grocery branding

One can observe similar patterns in the grocery business. Well-integrated, effective virtual supply chains are commonplace in the UK industry. Suppliers, who once dominated the market through their product brands, are now adjusting to a world wherein the retailers' brands offer consumers the bigger promise and now dominate the market. Suppliers' value added is no longer exclusively from the supply of strong national brands. Increasingly, it is based upon taking responsibility for optimizing the category assortment, managing their own inventory and supporting the overall marketing strategies of the retailer. If grocery manufacturers undertake such responsibilities in good faith, we can envisage a scenario wherein retailers form Level 3 partnerships with key suppliers in order to reduce cost, as well as allow them to focus on creating new value for the consumer.

We propose that the major retail chains have won the battle for efficient supply of food and related products to the household. Their UOVPs based upon superior performance, portfolio, network of relationships and reputation have beaten the disorganized collection of individual product brands' unique selling propositions. There are further enhancements to their winning formula in the pipeline. For example, effective consumer response and Internet-based shopping. In winning the battle for the supply chain, retailers have created a certain sameness to their value propositions, brands, stores, ranges and prices. Aside from their theme colors, it might be hard to distinguish between shopping in a Tesco, Sainsbury's or Safeway superstore.

However, the battle for differentiation and discovery of major new growth opportunities has already commenced. An area of interest seems to be in the bundling of diverse household products under the management of the retailer. We predict that food retailers will evolve into suppliers of a broad range of household services and products supported in their attack on new markets with superior data about their customer base.

The new markets already in the sights of the retailers include credit cards, savings, insurance, pensions, electricity, gas and water. As car makers are investing in their dealer networks as the focus of customer relationship management, retailers are betting on their loyalty schemes to provide them with the means to differentiate their offer and develop powerful relationships with their most profitable customers. Data, customization and selective reward for desired behavior are powerful tools with which to crack open new markets. Used properly, these tools will encourage consumers to treat retailers as preferred suppliers for grocery and related items akin to the relationship enjoyed between businesses in successful business-to-business relationships. The promiscuous shopper will be replaced with the partner–shopper seeking to take time and cost out of the supply of a broad range of household goods and services.

The broader the range of goods and services supplied by the retailer, the more the need for Level 3 and 4 partnerships and selective outsourcing of well-defined categories of product and service. Just as the automakers found in the 1980s that they could no longer do everything well, the retailers will reach a similar conclusion quickly. If their brand discriminators are to be found in the newer services, they will actively seek to devolve some of their traditional tasks to more focused suppliers. However, this effective third-party supplier base will tend to homogenize the look and feel of grocery retailing and force major retailers to move beyond price, selection and short checkout lines toward relationship management and effective customization of their service to individual households. Competition will be based upon a broad definition of organizational promises and in this light, Tesco's current tag line of "every bit helps" seems more attuned to UOVP thinking than Sainsbury's traditional promise of "good food costs less."

In the automotive industry, we suggested that component makers, largely unknown to consumers today, might invest in brand building to add value to the supply chain leader. The food industry has started from the opposite point: the "component" suppliers such as Unilever, P&G, Gillette, and Nestlé have created strong product brands that are valued by both retailers and households. The brand owners are looking to imitate the business-to-business component suppliers in channel cooperation (termed "category management" by the consumer goods giants), producing retailers' brands, supply chain optimization, and customization of promotional offers for each major retailer. Perhaps

Brand owners must accept their role as "component supplier" to the major retailers who appear set to dominate the future supply chain for household goods

there is a natural balance between brand building and being a good supplier which, regardless of industry, companies that do not dominate the supply chain must find.

This idea offers brand owners the prospect that some of the brands in which they have invested so heavily over the past 50 years will still have economic value. However, brand owners must accept their role as "component supplier" to the major retailers who appear set to dominate the future supply chain for household goods.

The role and process of managing customer relationships from the suppliers' perspective and the implementation issues surrounding partnership initiatives are discussed further in Chapter 8.

SUMMARY

In order to realign brand with customer value, the UOVP extends into the supply chain to facilitate the development of networks which create more customer value than those of competitors.

Traditional supply chain management existed in an environment characterized by sequential decision making and pre-determined component specification. Companies were managed as if they had all the resources needed to design and specify products and services down to a very fine level of detail. The specifications for components went to competing suppliers with an expectation that tendering for pre-determined parts drove costs down.

This arm's-length relationship with suppliers does not continue to serve companies well. Modern competition is based on rapid exploitation of opportunities, quick response to customers' increasing expectations, and experimentation with new technologies and techniques. Such rapid change in one's core products and services is hard enough in itself to manage. Few, if any, can drag a long supply chain with them as they move quickly from opportunity to opportunity.

Companies are moving to higher levels of supplier partnerships in order to increase their own ability to create customer value. We have identified four levels of supply partnership on a continuum:

- *Level 1* – Traditional supplier that has a transactional relationship with the brand owner. The supplier sells specified goods and services to the brand owner on the basis of price, service, and quality.
- *Level 2* – Supply chain optimizer that works in cooperation with the brand owner to reduce total cost (increase total benefit) of the brand's customer value proposition.
- *Level 3* – Supply chain partner that takes responsibility for a significant proportion of the brand's value delivery. Partners not only optimize the supply chain, they take some responsibility for innovation in their area of expertise.
- *Level 4* – Value chain partner that enables the brand to extend past its traditional competencies.

As companies move to these higher levels of supply partnerships, their partners increasingly contribute to the UOVP brand. This contribution is measured either through overt co-branding or by enabling the company to move its own UOVP to higher levels of customer value.

Further reading

Professor Martin Christopher in his book, *Logistics and Supply Chain Management*, provides a comprehensive appraisal of the role which the supply chain plays in creating competitive advantage. The book will be of particular interest to those in functional organizations trying to leverage this competitive advantage since he recommends that logistics can provide the necessary impetus for organizational change. The Xerox case study on implementing an integrator supply chain is very relevant to this chapter.

- Martin Christopher, *Logistics and Supply Chain Management*, Financial Times Pitman Publishing, London, 1992.

Richard Lamming is also a recognized authority on supply partnerships and the move toward lean supply and supplier-based innovation among manufacturers.

- Richard Lamming, *Beyond Partnership: Strategies for Innovation and Lean Supply*, Prentice Hall, London, 1993.

- Richard Lamming, "Squaring Lean Supply with Supply Chain Management," *International Journal of Operations and Production Management*, vol.16, no.2.

The Economic Intelligence Unit reports on supply chain management in Europe and refers to it as the new competitive battleground, as electronic data interchange and real-time supply become embedded.

- The Economic Intelligence Unit Research Report (0-85058-887-1), 1995.

ASSET MANAGEMENT

Asset management

INTRODUCTION

Creating a brand today necessitates the incorporation of a broader range of components into the brand promise than that anticipated by the architects of 4Ps marketing. We have outlined our view that the organization's product brands are no longer the total embodiment of customer value. The sharp edge of creating customer value lies elsewhere and many of the key drivers of customer value are buried within the assets of the corporation: its capabilities, knowhow, culture and methodologies. If these assets are among the most customer-relevant value creators today, asset management must contribute to the brand-building process. The UOVP is a tool for systematically directing the investment and management of corporate assets in service of the overall customer proposition.

WHAT DO WE MEAN BY ASSETS?

In Chapter 5, Supply Partnership, we dealt with the process by which organizations secure the inputs that they need for value creation. These supplies were defined to include physical goods and services as well as broader capabilities, such as managing credit, design expertise, or customer service methodologies.

Once supply partners deliver goods, services, or capabilities, the organization will then transform them into outputs (that which it sells) by deploying a range of its own assets. In the next chapter we will look at the transformation or production process itself, but here we are interested in the assets deployed against the inputs in their transformation process.

In a typical manufacturing environment, the assets would include physical plant and equipment (machinery). However, we do not want to limit our discussion of assets to the physical because in the knowledge-based environment, the key assets deployed against inputs are knowhow, patents and procedures. For example, an advertising agency buys consumer research from behavioral psychologists as supply partners and then deploys its own methodologies and tools to process these supplies into a finished advertisement. This transformation process is often called the creative process and the assets involved with it are knowhow, frameworks, methodologies and, of course, people.

Our definition of assets therefore includes the tangible items of plant, equipment and location as well as the intangibles of knowhow, patents and brand names. We consider that a well-known brand is an intangible asset akin to other forms of intellectual property. To the extent that one can extract an economic rent from it or use it to launch into new ventures, the brand is a valuable asset.

Assets, as we have defined them, represent the stock of the organization's capabilities. We therefore maintain that the management of the assets can no longer be the exclusive domain of functional departments wherein those assets normally reside. They must be managed to deliver the organization's differentiated, value added proposition to customers. Even more than traditional strategy and planning, the UOVP will help organizations to understand this better and build the assets to take on more of a "front seat" in the drive to build business and create customer value.

> *The management of corporate assets has too often been guided by cost measures to the exclusion of value*

The traditional approach to asset management

In our experience, the management of corporate assets has too often been guided by cost measures to the exclusion of value. Asset managers are measured on the total cost of providing a corporate service or the cost per customer. The problem with this approach is that it fails to develop the real capabilities within the organization that long term will enable it to differentiate itself from competitors.

The authors worked for Unilever during a period when a key performance measure for its detergent factories was the cost per ton to produce laundry detergent. It was an effective and simple measure of the performance of Unilever's numerous factories worldwide. This cost-per-ton approach seemed to apply irrespective of the different retail prices and profit margins for different brands produced. The way in which Unilever moved its managers between countries and businesses ensured that this mindset was not limited to detergents. As markets grew more competitive, marketing was challenged to be more ambitious and innovative. It began to plan for more sophisticated and complex product offers and cost-per-ton thinking was destined to clash with innovation.

We remember an instance where marketers were demanding more customization of the product range while manufacturing and commercial were following a global policy of product harmonization. There was conflict between marketing's desire for flexibility, experimentation and customization, and manufacturing's strategy of long, undifferentiated production runs. In a moment of frustration with his factory's reluctance to modify a product, a Unilever marketing manager exclaimed, "I do not believe that our policy of low-cost manufacturing is about cheaply producing goods that consumers no longer wish to buy and we no longer wish to sell." Fortunately, the manager's argument won the day, a testament to the quality and good sense of Unilever's people.

Corporate IT managers often evaluate their department's performance on measures of throughput, the cost per million instructions processed (MIP). We would argue that the value of IT no longer lies in its ability to crunch numbers quickly. IT creates value in the organization when it helps it to develop a profound understanding of the capabilities of information technology and of all that is required to exploit its potential. In the best companies, IT is often a catalyst for reinventing customer value, business process improvement, and improving organization structures. The appropriate measures of performance should help IT explore electronic commerce, align information systems to the goals of the business, and achieve the right balance between business benefit and technology investment. Managers of data centers with world-class MIP performance are often dismayed when their organizations hire consultants or outsourcers to dig for the value hidden within the company's IT assets.

Similarly, customers have a different definition of value from telephone call centers than that used by many call center managers. One of the fastest growing areas of customer service is telephone-based call centers and, increasingly, it is the tool of choice for helping customers solve problems with the organization's service or products.

Customers derive value from a company's call center when their problem is solved. Call centers are often managed to deliver throughput, not successful resolution of customer problems. Measures of performance usually include number of calls handled per hour, number of rings before answering and the speed at which enquiries cycle through the organization. The journey for a customer begins with the first line of contact staff who qualifies the enquiry and hands over to the appropriate second line of service provider, who may need to hand off to a third line service provider. Demand simulations allow managers to allocate manpower through the day and trade off between staff (cost) and the probability of meeting throughput measures. To maximize asset utilization, customers must join fair queues for the first line of contact staff and each subsequent line of service provider. Where the customer enquiries can easily be handled successfully by the service providers, this system appears to utilize the service center asset efficiently. However, a significant percentage of customer requests are not resolved in the first call and unfortunate customers must reconnect to the system in the same fair queue and loop through the process repeatedly. Many call centers cannot allow one service provider to see the customer through to problem resolution. While call center assets must be cost efficient, they must be effective at quickly solving customers' problems. The traditional focus on asset utilization over customer

> *It is rarely the fault of asset managers for managing the means and not the ends*

satisfaction reminds us of the old joke about the surgeon who claimed that, "The operation was a success, too bad the patient died."

It is rarely the fault of asset managers for managing the means and not the ends. What was the reward structure of Unilever plant managers that drove this cost-per-ton focus? One can sympathize with IT managers benchmarking MIP because it is measurable and they are constantly asked to "cost justify" individual programs when many investments provide benefits that are not easily quantified. How many call centers have adequate resources with which to define and deliver to customers' expectations?

Sales and marketing have long been the "rainmakers" of the organization and take priority for scarce resources. Asset managers must make do with the remaining resources yet it is often the case that the key capabilities needed to support the UOVP stem from these assets: knowhow, customer service centers, research, and employee development. Marketing's traditional focus on product strategy and branding has not equipped it for custodianship of its corporations' key capabilities and assets. Such assets and capabilities may prove to be more effective differentiators than anything contained in the marketing plan.

THE USE OF ASSETS IN BRAND BUILDING

UOVP thinking will encourage companies to align their asset management policies with the value that they wish to create in the market. In so doing, it will shift the focus from cost toward customer value.

Many leading companies have been practicing this for years and we would cite them as excellent examples of using assets to build their organization's proposition. In such companies, directors of these assets – be they stores, factories, IT, or corporate universities – look beyond the measures of asset utilization and performance and make decisions that "feel right" for the business. We have chosen three case studies to illustrate the point:

- Motorola's university
- Virgin's brand
- McDonald's franchising knowhow.

Motorola University (MU)

In the 1970s Motorola faced enormous difficulties competing with Japanese consumer electronics firms in its core business of radios and televisions. Like so many other American firms at that time, the Japanese ability to combine quality, innovation, design, and low price seemed to be unbeatable. Motorola shifted its marketplace strategy away from selling consumer electronics toward newer, high-technology markets such as mobile phones and semi-conductors where it felt it could recreate competitive advantage.

This shift to higher technology and increased product sophistication had practical implications for a company used to making low-cost radios. Early on, the board realized that its workforce lacked the skills and, in some cases, the basic literacy required to run the more sophisticated manufacturing processes necessary for quality produc-tion of high-technology products. The company accepted that it would upgrade its workforce and management commensurate with the new strategy.

Motorola University (MU) was created to meet the need for retrain-ing and skills development. It became an important enabler of the new marketplace strategy and took a very broad view of education and development. It developed world-class capabilities in teaching total quality management, process control, and other aspects of what became known as "six sigma quality" to support the new business strategy. It also offered courses in other areas of interest to its staff and became accredited to offer engineering degrees.

Motorola successfully entered, and indeed now dominates, many of the targeted new markets. Its transformation from mass market car radios and televisions to semi-conductors, mobile phones, cellular infrastructure and computers is a case history of corporate transfor-mation. The company is now regarded as a leading proponent of qual-ity manufacturing, innovation, and skills development. Without the astute management of the University, would the company have suc-ceeded?

As the challenges facing Motorola change, the MU adds new courses and capabilities to meet the business needs. The markets for Motorola's products are fast becoming global and consumer led. By way of example, in the mid-1990s small office and home purchases of computers exceeded that of corporations by volume. In an ironic twist of fate, Motorola left the consumer goods business for high-tech-nology and now the high-technology business is becoming a con-sumer electronics business. Aware of the implications for its business, MU is at the forefront of equipping management for the new core competencies it must have: global marketing, branding and retailer management.

Motorola is not alone in having a corporate university. However, it is distinguished by the extent to which it is used throughout the business and not just as a training and development vehicle.

For example, when Motorola recently negotiated a joint venture with Siemens, part of its offer was that it undertook to provide training in quality manufacturing. Siemens is a vital partner for Motorola in Germany, but it also competes with it across some product categories. Accepting training from a company with whom one competes is a bold move, but it clearly demonstrates the power of the organization's asset in developing an organization value proposition for the market. Quality is an important component of Motorola's offer to business customers and MU a key contributor to the brand.

Recently Motorola sponsored a major study into the attitudes of the British public to new technologies. When the executive team in charge of the study decided to host a conference in order to share the results, it immediately thought to ask the Vice-President of the University to anchor the presentation. The University is one of the company's greatest marketing assets.

MU extends its reach past Motorola into its suppliers and has trained a vast number of Motorola's suppliers. The University has become an important part of supplier partnership management.

In these ways, the role of the University has expanded since its inception from organization development through to customer development, marketing and supply chain management. It receives the funding and support commensurate to its contribution throughout the business and not just that of a training center. Its directors see their role as part of the business development process and work closely with line management to ensure that the University is aligned to the brand and the company's customer value proposition.

From the perspective of the UOVP, a major component of the Motorola brand is its reputation for quality products. This reputation transcends the company's current markets served and allows it to participate or lead the innovation of new markets. The core processes that support quality are as much a part of the brand as they are of sound manufacturing practice. We have no doubt that quality manufacturing is the result of effective manufacturing processes. However, it must be acknowledged that the knowhow was incubated within the asset of Motorola University and that this asset is itself a major component of the marketing of Motorola.

Virgin

Few brands have generated as much discussion among marketers as Virgin, the creation of the charismatic Richard Branson, self-styled slayer of the dragons within corporate establishment. We have been told that the brand name Virgin represents a statement from its founder that his organization will be a newcomer to each business it enters. In consequence, Virgin's business portfolio will make little sense to the traditional marketing strategist. Following its highly successful competition and legal wrangle with British Airways over transatlantic business, it has moved into businesses as diverse as recording, retail, computers, drinks, beauty products, financial services and travel. It has not been successful in all of its ventures and yet the brand reputation does not seem to have been harmed. The market has given Virgin the permission to experiment and fail.

A more traditional approach to marketing would have Virgin leveraging its product market shares and learning across contiguous product markets and entering into extensive licensing arrangements abroad. The record companies with which it once competed have tended to remain within the entertainment markets. Its airline rivals do not venture out much past vacation packages. Its largest soft drink competitor agonized over the decision to launch Diet Coke.

No doubt the character of Virgin's founder, Richard Branson, explains much of the corporate strategy and brand reputation. One can post-rationalize the Virgin track record from the UOVP perspective and judge the UOVP upon its prediction as to where the business will be successful in the future.

We would suggest that the Virgin (UOVP) brand is based upon its reputation for integrity and transparency as well as its performance in delivering better-than-expected service.

We observe the development of two key strands to its brand strategy:

- Virgin looks to reinvent customer value in the market by taking out non-value-adding costs and providing the consumer with greater transparency of costs. This seems to be the key to its financial services and soft drink businesses.

- Virgin offers a higher quality service versus industry norms and delivers it through a highly motivated workforce. This is a key to the success of Virgin Airline and of Eurostar – the high-speed passenger rail link running under the English Channel.

The Virgin UOVP architecture is shown in Fig. 6.1.

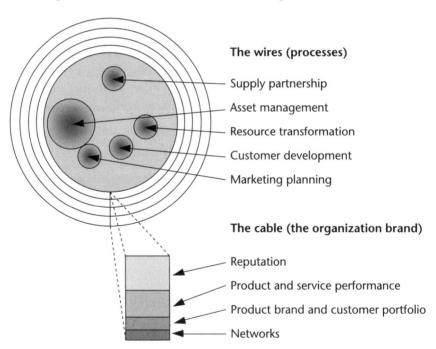

The wires (processes)

Supply partnership

Asset management

Resource transformation

Customer development

Marketing planning

The cable (the organization brand)

Reputation

Product and service performance

Product brand and customer portfolio

Networks

Fig. 6.1 The Virgin UOVP architecture

In UOVP nomenclature, the brand mix is heavily weighted toward the reputation and service performance components. Of the core processes that support this mix, asset management is the most prominent. Virgin deploys its two key assets (brand and its service knowhow) to compete with established players and create a unique customer proposition.

Unlike many competitors to dominant organizations in newly deregulated markets, Virgin's airline business does not compete on price. It offers a different type of in-flight experience. Using an analogy with the film studio world, Virgin's cabin "directors" are working with a different script than that used by British Airways and they try to create a different movie. The script, its unique service knowhow, is the property of Virgin and its ability to show its film on every flight is one of its key service performance brand differentiators.

The Virgin "movie" plays well to some rail audiences too. Virgin, part owner of the channel tunnel passenger rail operator, Eurostar, has recreated its airplane service ambience on rails. Staff appear to be motivated and valued by Eurostar; they provide the customer with a superior service to that experienced elsewhere on British trains. Regular users of the British Rail service between Manchester and London were overjoyed with the awarding of that line to Virgin. They expect that Virgin will recreate rail travel experience in its image over time.

Virgin is also using a different script when it makes "movies" in the financial services markets. The company's long-term financial savings products offer greater transparency of charges throughout the sales and delivery process than those of its competitors. Virgin leverages its reputation for integrity by offering simple products that are differentiated by having clearly stated charges. The established players have a different script: one that suggests that long-term savings are very complicated and that one must engage well-paid advisors to help one choose.

Not all of the brand's movies succeed at the box office. Virgin's entry into the computing market was short lived and it has failed to make a real impact upon the drinks market. We would speculate that, in these markets, Virgin's brand mix of reputation and service performance may not be an automatic recipe for success. For example, companies that prosper in personal computers tend to build their brand upon product portfolio expertise and a network of alliances that ensure their solutions are well integrated into corporate IT architectures. There are few opportunities for Virgin's service model to work at the hardware level and there is sufficient transparency within the industry for that not to be a differentiator.

Given its history and management, we should expect Virgin to surprise with bold new ventures. However, the UOVP analysis of Virgin predicts that it will be most successful where it can add value through differentiated service using a motivated workforce. Perhaps restaurants, amusement/holiday parks or book selling?

Retail franchises – McDonald's

We would claim that retail franchise brands in fast food, printing, and car repair businesses are built upon effective asset management. For McDonald's, managing assets such as brand, store design, and food preparation knowhow, delivers the majority of its brand and customer value. Marketing at McDonald's is more about managing the assets than it is about the 4Ps.

In the case of McDonald's, we would describe the UOVP brand as follows:

- reputation: family fun, value for money, hygiene
- performance: consistency in taste of food, speed of service, cleanliness of restaurants
- portfolio: clear product portfolio strategy based upon burgers, fries and soft drinks, and a customer portfolio of families with young children.

- networks: Disney for joint promotion
  co-branded:
  - Cadbury's Flake in its ice cream desserts (UK)
  - Coca-Cola has been introduced through branding at point of sale and on paper cups.

Much has been written about the McDonald's service model and how it was an innovator in business process design. While not minimizing the importance of all of its business processes, this chapter focuses on the use of its assets to deliver its proposition. We maintain that asset management is perhaps the most important business process a branded franchisor such as McDonald's uses in delivering the brand. The key assets that we consider McDonald's uses are brand name, brand properties, store design, and Hamburger University.

The brand-related assets – the name, the Ronald McDonald character and the golden arches – are powerful communicators of the UOVP and major contributors to McDonald's success. The reaction of Muscovites to the first McDonald's in the former USSR is evidence of this.

The brand is also an instrument for attracting high quality managers. The brand acts as an endorsement of business and financial success. Attracting high-quality managers is essential for any service business looking to create high standards across thousands of locations. Such managers are attracted by a strong brand, and it helps managers manage expectations for their delivery.

> Asset management is perhaps the most important business process a branded franchisor such as McDonald's uses in delivering the brand

One of the keys to the success of any franchised operation such as McDonald's is the consistency of delivery throughout the world. Every one of its thousands of outlets must meet a high standard of hygiene, fun environment, speed of service, and friendliness. McDonald's ensures that it can deliver that consistency by training its people to a common standard at Hamburger University. It is interesting that while the corporate university at Motorola is a catalyst of change and business development, Hamburger University is more an instrument of operational control for McDonald's. In both organizations, customer value is created by the integration of the university into the brand.

Another major contributor to the consistency of delivery is the store design, again a core asset of McDonald's; its knowhow in store design is obvious value to customer and franchisee. In the UK, McDonald's has its own in-house design team who update continuously its standard store designs as well as create site-specific designs in architecturally sensitive locations. The store design, training, and the brand are necessary to the success of McDonald's and it has always integrated the management of these vital assets into the development of its overall consumer proposition.

The brand is an instrument for attracting high-quality managers

TOWARD A SYSTEMATIC APPROACH TO ASSET MANAGEMENT

There are many examples of businesses using their assets in imaginative ways in order to create customer value; the case studies just examined do not provide a comprehensive list. Companies with extensive retail networks are looking to leverage them. Branch network banks are reconsidering their assets in a digital age. Gasoline retailers are considering how to repackage their network of retailers as a delivery capability for Internet-based retailing and reposition their brands as convenience outlets. Computer manufacturers are leveraging knowhow to participate in the growing market for consulting and reposition themselves as solutions providers.

Unfortunately, there does not appear to be a widely accepted systematic means by which companies can release more of their assets to the creation of customer value. As managers, we are left with anecdotes, but little in the way of systematic methodology and tools with which to work. In the absence of an overall framework, the shift in asset management from a cost focus to value creation is difficult. Asset owners are generally not empowered to lead such transformation. Marketing is unsure about allowing it to happen. Measurement and reward systems discourage it.

The traditional approach to marketing planning tends to create a business development strategy that is disjointed from the asset base of the company. The business development tends to be generated, in the plan at least, through new products, new sales initiatives, acquisitions and alliances. Asset management is derived from the business winning strategies in the plan and asset managers comply with the dictates of the plan rather than shape the plan itself. For strategists still working within the dictates of product-centered value, the "ideal" product portfolio is created without the "constraints" of the existing company and delivered by a low-cost combination of internal and external sources. In this environment, we believe that companies continually underinvest in the development of their assets and capabilities.

The UOVP and the framework for asset management

We believe that the UOVP can provide the necessary framework for companies to consider asset management in a far more strategic and customer-directed way than they do now. The UOVP architecture makes the role of assets in the delivery of the customer proposition obvious by asking managers to:

- recreate the value chain in which they compete
- free asset management from the constraints of product planning
- create structure and purpose to empowerment.

Recreate the value chain

UOVP planning starts with the overall industry value chain and not a series of individual product markets. It encourages companies to recreate the value chain in which they operate and not merely to participate within it. Such discontinuous change is often led by those in control of the corporate capabilities and assets, not by the marketers.

For example, inventors, not product market strategies, drive SONY; we have all heard of the mythology surrounding the invention and commercialization of the Walkman. The mission statement of SONY talks about creating an environment where engineers and visionaries will thrive, not about dominating any specific market.

At First Direct, Britain's first major telephone bank, information technology does not merely automate the inefficient practices of traditional financial services companies. New technology and business processes fundamentally change how customer value is created and delivered. IT is now a powerful creative force and progressive companies are creating digital business strategies around their evolving IT assets. Those at the cutting edge of such thought can imagine possibilities that do not respect traditional definitions of market, customer and price. In such a world, the knowhow associated with the IT function cannot allow its investment program to be dictated by the here-and-now limitations of traditional product portfolio management.

Free asset management from constraints of product planning

Would Motorola University have been created if it had had to be "cost justified" on the basis of the marketing plan of any single business unit or product market strategy? Yet, without MU, one could argue that many of the Motorola product successes would have been compromised. The impetus for the program came from an organization proposition.

Was the over $100 million investment for "Intel Inside" advertising cost justified through incremental volume? Or did the senior management understand that as IT becomes a consumer good, an investment in a brand asset was necessary?

In our experience, the development of organization assets are often held hostage to the needs of an individual business case. In such cases, managers tend to cut the cloth to fit the suit and the asset is compromised almost by design.

For example, most toiletries companies have expensive programs to build endorsement from key professional groups. L'Oréal carefully cultivates its image and support among hair stylists for its hair products and amortizes that investment across a wide portfolio of products sold under its house name. It is highly successful in a wide range of hair products: shampoo, styling aids, and colorants. On the other hand, its worldwide rival, Unilever, has traditionally focused on stand-alone product brands. As it is rare for one product to be able to support a similar program to L'Oréal, its brands are less likely to enjoy a similar level of implicit or explicit expert endorsement. Unilever's successes in haircare have been strongest in shampoos/conditioners where stand-alone product brands dominate. In this chicken

> *Empowering all managers to add more value to customers will prove to be more productive than the "initiativitis" that grips many companies today*

and egg situation, it is most effective when the entire company commits to a corporate asset and stakes its reputation upon it. Failure to do so may limit one's ability to participate fully in a market.

The UOVP removes asset management from the strait-jacket of the product plan and allows the company to consider its overall proposition to the customer and the processes needed to support it.

Structure and purpose to empowerment

Perhaps most importantly, UOVP planning provides the next level of detail and structure to empowerment as preached by the management gurus. The anecdotes of companies using assets imaginatively may prove inspirational to those managing their IT functions, service centers or corporate universities. The problem of management is what to do when empowered managers bump against one another.

The UOVP provides a blueprint for all managers to visualize the extent and nature of their potential contribution to the customer value proposition. It provides a common language and understanding of what is important to the customer and where the company is going to differentiate itself from competitors. Against that understanding, empowering all managers to add more value to customers will prove to be more productive than the "initiativitis" that grips many companies today.

SUMMARY

There is a wide range of corporate assets that can potentially make a substantial contribution to the UOVP brand. These include traditional physical assets such as plant and equipment but increasingly include knowhow, brands and culture – the intangible assets.

Traditionally assets have been managed for cost and utilization measures creating efficiency but not necessarily excellence. UOVP planning encourages a shift in asset management from cost optimization focus to value creation.

Many companies already use their assets as powerful components of their organization brands: Motorola University, the Virgin brand and service know-how and McDonald's brand, design and knowhow.

UOVP planning creates a systematic approach to the transformation of assets into powerful components of brand building. It urges the company to consider the entire customer value proposition and not just marketing. The UOVP frees asset managers from the narrow confines of supporting individual product marketing initiatives and allows the company to develop the capabilities needed to support its overall proposition in the market. Finally, UOVP architecture provides some context and purpose to empowering managers within the company so that empowerment does not lead to chaos and conflict.

Further reading

This chapter has been influenced primarily by our consultancy work and discussions with senior management about their changing approach to asset management. However, with regard to the brand asset, our thinking has been reinforced by John Murphy's book, *Brand Valuation*, particularly in the context of internal transfer costing based on the brand asset.

- John Murphy (ed.), *Brand Valuation*, 2nd edn, Business Books Ltd, London, 1991.

For those interested in finding out more about Motorola University (MU) we recommend William Wiggenhorn's article in *Harvard Business Review*.

- William Wiggenhorn, "Motorola U: When Training Became an Education," *Harvard Business Review*, July–August, pp 71–83, 1990.

James Quin's book, *Intelligent Enterprise*, provides a very interesting perspective on knowledge management within the organization and establishes management knowhow as a key company asset.

- James Quin, *Intelligent Enterprise*, Free Press, New York, 1992.

RESOURCE
TRANSFORMATION

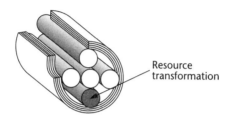

Resource
transformation

INTRODUCTION

Our definition of resource transformation – the ability to effectively trans-form supplies and assets into goods and services that customers wish to buy – has long been recognized as the most vital component of creating value. Perhaps no subject area in recent times has been the focus of so much management study; total quality (TQ), business process reengineering (BPR), Kaizen, Kanban and JIT have dominated the corporate agenda for much of the past decade. There can be no doubt that improved resource transformation processes have created real customer value through improved product quality, reduced total costs and increased choice for customers.

Marketing, with its traditional focus on the 4Ps and product planning, has largely ignored and hence has been sidelined by these programs. In fact, many consultants with whom we work comment that marketing can be the most obstructive department in change programs. At the root of this obstructiveness is not merely personality or status: there is a fundamental difference in belief as to what creates customer value. Marketing has been trained to act as the value creator through its knowledge of price, advertising and positioning, while process-based change agents look to reduce costs, time and defects throughout the supply chain. It

> **The challenge for reengineering in the future is to integrate brand differentiation with process improvement**

is the latter group of managers that is in the ascendency in the corporate world.

In the 1980s and early 1990s, we maintain that most American and European companies needed a healthy dose of such process-based change. Looking back, we realize that their manufacturing was costly and poor in quality compared to Japanese competitors, services failed to satisfy increasingly demanding customers and innovation was often either too late or off *the mark. No one book so powerfully describes these problems (and their cure) than Hammer and Champy's* Reengineering the Corporation. *Most companies with which we work have integrated much of the authors' thinking into their management culture since the book was published in 1993.*

As we close the 1990s, however, we observe that effective resource transformation processes, while necessary for success, are themselves no longer sufficient. As most companies now embrace process management, some feel that they are on a reengineering treadmill of constantly reducing costs and working faster just to stay even with the competition. Resource transformation itself does not necessarily recreate the customer preference and differentiation of traditional brand building.

The challenge for reengineering in the future is to integrate brand differentiation with process improvement. We believe that the UOVP provides this framework because it explicitly links the organization brand with its core business processes.

We now go on to look at the limitations of the traditional resource transformation in vertical organizations.

THE TRADITIONAL APPROACH TO RESOURCE TRANSFORMATION

The traditional approach to transforming resources into goods and services is too sequential and functionally driven to create value commensurate with that demanded by the marketplace today. A very simplified feedback loop, illustrated in Fig. 7.1, demonstrates the sequential nature of fulfilling customer needs with current and new products across functional divisions.

Traditionally, marketing and sales act as arbiters of customer needs and instruct their organization's resource transformation functions, such as manufacturing, logistics, or distribution, accordingly. These functions then instruct those in charge of purchasing, who, in turn,

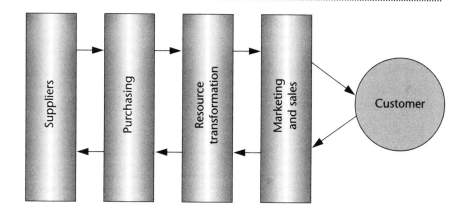

Fig. 7.1 Sequential processing

instruct suppliers. On the way back, the information about customer needs is handled through the same chain of events. Rapid and interactive customer problem solving is complicated by the functional divisions between each stage of the process. This is as true for the process of fulfilling customer needs with existing goods and services (fulfillment) as it is for creating new goods and services (new product development (NPD)).

Figure 7.1 could be expanded to separate marketing and sales, thus adding one more filter to customer information. It could also include several layers of suppliers, each of whom operate within their own functional hierarchies. Companies that map their information and physical product flows through their systems are shocked by the complexity with which they conduct their business and how far removed customers become.

The management literature is replete with examples of this. Hammer and Champy provide excellent examples in their book. No doubt each reader will have similar anecdotes from their own experiences. The authors' favorite involves a package color selection and verification process for which a company allowed 16 weeks. It transpired that two days was actually sufficient when all the right people were in one room for two or three hours at the start. The other 15 weeks and 3 days were spent handing off papers and samples between departments and companies.

Such sequential information processing from customers and within the supply chain burdens the customer with unnecessary costs and lengthy delays while increasing the possibility of misinterpretation. As children, we have all played the game called "broken telephone," where a message is whispered through a chain of friends and ends up amusingly different from the original. As children it was fun – as businesses it is costly and inefficient.

New product development in such functionally driven environments often fails. Truly innovative ideas that represent real breakthroughs in customer value are rarely produced in a sequential fashion where every activity is filtered through functional hierarchies. The effort required to implement even the slightest improvement in the customer offer through such a system is often just too time consuming for most managers, and what does get through is often bland and "me-too." Managing the political process gets more priority than managing the real outcome; we do things right instead of doing the right things. Many of the best run bureaucracies, often highly admired companies, find that they are never first to the market with innovations. Many such firms patch up their broken processes, through skunk works and acquisitions but never really address the root of their problems.

Such problems are equally manifest in the processes through which companies fulfill customer needs with their current product and service portfolios. Poor quality, unmet demands for customization, deficient services, and the lack of interoperability with other parts of the customer's solution are rarely addressed in an effective manner. It is only with the greatest of effort, by threats and complaining, that customers can get these issues resolved. It is not that people are unwilling to help, it is that they are operating within the constraints of functional organizations unable to mobilize their full resources to fix customer problems.

Most companies would accept this critique and are transforming their functional structures and sequential tasking to resource transformation that is managed as a process using a management structure that follows the work flows from customers through the supply chain.

THE NEW APPROACH – MANAGE PROCESSES NOT FUNCTIONS

Battered by two decades of OPEC-induced inflation and Japanese and Korean competition, western businesses were ready for radical solutions and embraced a rapid succession of process-centered management techniques with which we are all familiar: TQ, Kaizen, JIT, Kanban, and BPR.

Despite some detractors decrying management fads and consultancy-led change, there is not a long line of companies wishing to recreate the functional organizations which have been replaced by flatter structures that support process management. While each of the techniques has certain unique characteristics, there are some underlying principles that seem to be part of every process management solution.

Cross-functional business processes

Despite the best efforts of many well-managed companies and the goodwill of their managers, it is increasingly difficult to achieve breakthrough improvements in time, speed and cost across functional divisions.

The organization must turn to face customer needs directly through the management of its core processes and should not be based upon an outdated model of sequential resource transformation.

Over the past decade, companies have begun to understand their processes of creating customer value and to describe them from the customer's viewpoint. These processes typically include order fulfill-ment, credit approval, system installation and customer problem solving. They cut across the organization's existing functions, such as marketing, sales, production, service and procurement. Therefore, organizations have restructured around business processes rather than functions. Someone (usually the process owner) needs to be accountable to the customer for the entire process and measured on their perceptions of performance.

End-to-end visibility of processes

The process owners described above need different structures and information with which to manage their businesses. They must be able to "see" their process from deep within the supply chain through to the customer. The purchasing department can no longer act as the single source of contact between the company and its suppliers. Sim-ilarly, sales cannot monopolize customer relationships. Process own-ers need to network as much outside their organizations as within because it is important to build effective working relationships with their counterparts throughout the supply chain.

Breakthrough improvements are most likely to happen when process owners lead initiatives between suppliers, manufacturers and distributors that remove cost and time from the entire value chain.

In almost every industry, companies are aligning themselves to global supply chains. These supply chains are being "wired" together with sophisticated new information technology that allows individ-ual companies to look forward and backward through this chain with perfect visibility. As retailers sell their goods, the information is automatically transmitted throughout the supply chain to ensure replenishment without inventories building up at each level. As airplanes are scheduled to fly, spares and services are dynamically reconfigured to ensure the right resource is at the right place at the right time. Everywhere, managers are working within end-to-end networks enabled

> *In almost every industry, companies are aligning themselves to global supply chains*

through information sharing. The feedback loop illustrated by Fig. 7.1 is replaced by processes pipes through the organization allowing the company to react to customer needs in real time.

Service culture

Process-driven organizations with end-to-end visibility have created a situation whereby customer-facing staff now have the ability to redirect the entire supply chain to meet customers' individual needs. We have moved from an economy of "make and sell" to one of "listen and serve."

The classic case of make and sell was the car industry. Long production lines to achieve economies of scale created massive inventories that had to be pushed out to the public. Today, sales representatives and customers direct the supply chain using dealers' computers to customize cars which are then scheduled for future production. Customers get the car they

> *We have moved from an economy of "make and sell" to one of "listen and serve"*

want to buy rather than a confusing choice of models that happen to be on the dealers' lots when they go to buy.

As Internet-based shopping becomes more prevalent, the customer's PC will take control of the car supply chain. Customers will work directly with their preferred suppliers on-line to develop solutions which meet their needs and then place orders through their keyboards. The solutions will be reconfigured on demand and the cost and supply chain implications worked out in real time. Everyone in this environment will be in the customer service business.

However, we must also accept that not everyone in the organization wishes to be in the customer service business. Professional pride, status and a sense of functional expertise make many people more comfortable within their old functionally defined job. Banks, telephone companies, gas companies and electricity suppliers are all working very hard to install service ethics and cultures within their organizations through change management programs. The successful companies from within these industries have focussed on culture change for very long periods of time.

DIFFERENTIATE RESOURCE TRANSFORMATION FOR BRANDING PURPOSES

When value was embodied within the product, the brand was built upon the core functionality of the offer. Now that value is created from business processes, companies must try to differentiate their resource transformation processes.

We have already referred to Cadillac winning the Baldrige award for quality while the public decided that they did not really wish to buy GM's cars. Clearly the aim of process management must be to create customer value; isolating process improvement from the marketplace is not a sensible strategy. In their enthusiasm to embrace TQ and BPR, some companies confused the means with the end.

To create value, resource transformation must be tied to a customer value proposition that is unique to the organization and relevant to customers. We now describe two such case studies taken from the computer industry.

Dell Computer

Dell Computer has effectively branded its production process to carve out a long-term, defensible position in arguably one of the world's toughest markets.

It sells personal computers and servers that are composed of industry standard components available to any competitor. Savage price competition leaves little room for sustainable price advantage with its competitors, many of whom are bigger and most likely enjoy superior economies of scale. Most of the customer value in a PC lies in the software; the hardware is almost a commodity. Yet, even in such an unfavorable environment, Dell continues to gain share almost every year and increase its profitability.

Dell succeeds by virtue of its ability to sell hundreds of thousands of computers every year, each built specially to meet individual customers' configuration of hardware and software. The company has pioneered mass customization for PCs and servers and successfully defends its share against imitators of its business model.

Traditional competitors design, produce, distribute and sell their PCs in sequence. They must estimate demand well in advance of production, gather orders from their channels to market and produce sufficient quantities to fill the pipeline. Because computer technology advances quickly, at times they inadvertently load their channels with "older" technology that is difficult to sell on to their final customers. The sequential nature of meeting customer needs increases both inventories through the supply chain and, hence, the likelihood of a seller holding the wrong inventory.

Dell sells directly to its customers and assembles to order from industry standard components. There is no inventory of finished goods, or middle men between Dell and the customer. Dell's resource transformation model removes non-value-adding inventory and distribution costs from the system. It also allows the customer to develop a direct relationship with the manufacturer. This combination of efficiency and customer intimacy was a real breakthrough in the market; Dell quickly became the largest "brand" among the direct suppliers. Its success is not due to its asset management for it has little in the way of superior design or intellectual property. Its supplier partners, such as Microsoft and Intel, sell branded components that are available to all its competitors. We attribute its success directly to its ability to incorporate its resource transformation process into its brand and value proposition.

Dell has been true to its value proposition and in a well-publicized move a few years ago, withdrew from selling computers through third party retailers such as computer superstores. This was a brave move given that retail was the fastest growing channel at that time. Internet commerce will only strengthen Dell's hand as it has already mastered dealing directly with hundreds of thousands of customers. Dell's web site now allows customers to configure their computers directly, taking even more time and cost out of the system. By defining its business on the basis of business processes, Dell's proposition remains unique and continues to add value.

Novell

Novell is an IT company that positioned itself in the market through a new process by which complex computer networking solutions were delivered to customers. Its process for manufacturing solutions was faster, more responsive and produced higher quality results less expensively than its competitors. Novell not only led the value chain in its market, but it successfully branded it to ensure that the benefits of its reengineering were more than transitory.

Before the advent of distributed computing, desktop terminals communicated with each other largely through mainframe or mini-computers. Effectively, the market for inter-desktop communication was dominated by enterprise systems from companies like IBM and Digital. With the growth of PCs, an opportunity was created for more peer-to-peer communications directly between PCs. Novell was a start-up created around one solution in what became known as the local area network (LAN) market.

Big systems hardware companies responded by offering customers layers of account management, after-sales services, upgrades and proprietary or near-proprietary systems. Managing such total solutions globally proved complex and expensive. Large-scale management structures and extensive processes grew around their sales and service organizations in order to manage the complexity. However, integrated solution providers could guarantee global reach, ownership of customer problem, and consistent service. As the installation of LANs was very complex, one would have thought the big systems model were well suited for this new opportunity.

Novell could not hope to emulate its competitors' resources. Instead it created a virtual organization through thousands of Value Added Resalers (VARs). These are normally small organizations that install and maintain specialized computer applications or industry solutions. Novell's value network was much less expensive to create and manage and offered arguably more responsive services through small, entrepreneurial VARs than the much larger, vertically integrated companies.

Unlike many software companies, Novell did not merely pass shrink-wrapped, branded products through its distribution channels. It created an extensive training program for its channels, down to the individual VAR engineer. After the explosion of LANs, Novell had certified over 40000 individual engineers and several thousand Novell engineer trainers within a few years. Its certified engineers proudly displayed their red Novell badges on their lapels. Certification was valuable to an engineer's personal prospects and to the VAR as a demonstration of its people's capability. By reaching out through several layers of distribution and "badging" the individual engineer, Novell branded the entire value chain and secured a market share in excess of 60 percent.

In recent years, Novell has faced a much more difficult challenge. Increasingly, its competitors are companies that are equally based in distributed computing and have powerful organization brand names such as Microsoft and Hewlett-Packard. Technology has also moved on with the popularization of the Internet. This will fundamentally change the way computers communicate with each other.

While we have not worked with Novell, we offer the observation that it seems to have defined its brand proposition too closely to the functionality of its LAN portfolio rather than its ability to deliver complex solutions, cheaper and better than competitors.

....

There are other well-known companies for whom we could ascribe the development of a successful UOVP due to an ability to differentiate their resource transformation processes. Examples include:

- **Toyota** whose UOVP of quality, reliability, and satisfied customers is a direct result of breakthroughs it made in the development of manufacturing processes (JIT, TQ).
- **Federal Express** branded the benefits of its breakthrough in package handling and is now trying to update that with the implementation of Internet access to their tracking systems.
- The **Casio** proposition is built around its low-cost manufacturing capability.
- **Swatch** brands a combination of its design knowhow with its low-cost manufacturing.

USING THE UOVP TO DIFFERENTIATE RESOURCE TRANSFORMATION

The UOVP is a useful tool for ensuring that the investments in process management contribute to the creation of differentiated customer value. It does so by encouraging companies to:

- build on the process knowhow that exists within the company
- free new product development from the constraints of traditional product portfolio planning
- institutionalize a real-time, customer service ethic through the company and its supply chain
- align UOVP and process improvement.

Build on process knowhow

Process owners within the business will react favorably and immediately to the UOVP toolset; they are already practicing much of it. In our work within companies, often the most prominent customer value creators have titles such as Logistics Director, Customer Services Director, Information Systems Director, Knowledge Manager and Director of People and Culture. These are the people who have developed intimate relationships with their counterparts in customer organizations down through the supply chain and work with them to create breakthrough achievements in speed, cost and quality. They have built powerful frontline teams of people around them to own and solve customer (internal or external) problems. They have minimized corporate "hand-offs" between groups so as to improve communications and responsiveness dramatically.

Process owners are looking for more leadership from their marketing and sales colleagues and will welcome the larger vision of customer value described in this book. As the traditional source of ideas on creating value, marketing and sales have largely eschewed process management and the gap between the leaders and the practitioners of customer value is growing. The UOVP will extend the benefits of looking end to end at customer value to those entrusted with the marketing and sales capabilities.

Free NPD from traditional product planning

At several points in the book we have made the point that for many companies, their NPD processes seem to be failing. This chapter attempts to demonstrate that lengthy, sequential processing of information between the value network and the customer is making innovation less effective and indeed timid. Top executives complain about the lack of really powerful new ideas originating from their organizations while retailers complain of "me-too" product ideas and meaningless line extensions on offer from the brand manufacturers. Few companies consistently redefine the markets in which they compete through innovative new ideas.

One of the problems companies face is that traditional product portfolio planning creates obstacles between the customer and the value adding processes

One of the problems companies face is that traditional product portfolio planning creates obstacles between the customer and the value adding processes. Product improvements are filtered via the portfolio planners, usually marketing and sales, which are then filtered through the supply chain and back again to customers.

The solution to this problem for most companies has been to redesign their organizations around core processes. We propose that the UOVP is the management tool needed to manage this shift from function- to process-centered product development within resource transformation.

Install a service ethic

Sometimes the process is the product. We have used examples of Toyota, Dell and Casio whose brands are essentially differentiated by the creation of excellent resource transformation processes. The same is perhaps even more true for professional service organizations. Advertising agencies sell the fruits of their individual creative processes; management consultancies tend to differentiate themselves on their "approach," i.e., the way they process information and create recommendations. Attempts at creating USPs for the "products" of professional service processes are often unsuccessful.

We suggest that both old and new product development increasingly happens interactively with the customer in "real time" rather than is the case within traditional, functionally driven companies. Process management avoids the sequential treatment of customer information and feedback illustrated in Fig. 7.1. People who join a real-time environment are less obsessed with product brand strategy and much more interested in adding value to customers every day. In the best organizations, everyone embraces the listen-and-serve mentality.

Marketing has often got in the way of such listen-and-serve mentality. Its training has been to architect the brand almost within a laboratory environment. The practice is far more analytical than the do-learn-do-learn mental processes of service cultures. The authors recently led a workshop for the top marketers of a large multinational where one participant described this as a "vision of hell." He felt far more comfortable continuing to develop product brands for his sales people to sell, than to work hand in glove with each major retailer as a category expert and facilitator.

Align customer value proposition and process improvement

Incorporating resource transformation directly into the customer value proposition will support the end-to-end nature of modern business processes.

UOVP architecture, as opposed to USP management, will ensure that process improvement supports the essential elements of the customer value proposition. It will tie together the elements of marketing planning, product development and customer service across core processes which are owned end to end by appropriate teams and which contribute directly to value creation.

SUMMARY

Resource transformation has been the focus of intense management development over the past decade, so much so that process management has replaced traditional strategy tools as the prime driver of business.

Marketing has largely ignored, and has been ignored by, the shift from function-driven to process-driven thinking. Marketers tend to work within an environment that is functionally based and processes information from customers through the supply chain in a sequential fashion. Marketing filters customer information and briefs resource transformation (production, logistics, service) to meet its interpretation of these needs. These asset managers then direct purchasing who, in turn, direct several layers of suppliers.

This sequential processing of customer information has created a situation where both product fulfillment and new product development are unresponsive to changes in customer need.

Most organizations have addressed this issue by redesigning themselves around core business processes, starting from the customer and ending deep in the supply chain. These end-to-end processes have provided companies with much greater visibility of the means by which they add value. This has helped them develop a service culture. Business has moved from "make and sell" to "listen and serve."

While the benefits of process-centered management are undeniable, it remains for companies to differentiate the way that their process improvements create value in a manner that is relevant to customers.

The UOVP helps companies brand their resource transformation by:

- building upon existing process knowhow
- freeing product development from the constraints of traditional brand management
- creating a service culture within the organization
- aligning processes to the UOVP.

Further reading

The definitive text on business resource transformation is Michael Hammer and James Champy's book, *Reengineering the Corporation*. When first introduced it produced a revolution in management thinking and process management and was very quickly placed high on the agenda within most corporations. As a result, the principle of flat-structured, process-centered organizations has become widely recognized as a central tenet for competing effectively.

- Michael Hammer and James Champy, *Reengineering the Corporation*, Harper Business, New York, 1993.

Quick-response innovation has provided outstanding results for those companies that reengineer their processes to be more responsive to their customers. George Stalk and Thomas Hout in their text, *Competing Against Time*, provide a very convincing argument for time-based competition.

- George Stalk and Thomas Hout, *Competing Against Time*, Free Press, New York, 1992.

Many of the functional management tasks were reviewed due to TQ management thinking which has led to further developments in process-based management. Leading texts on the subject of TQM are:

- J.S. Oakland, *Total Quality Management*, Heinemann Professional Series, Oxford, 1989.
- B.J. LaLonde and P.H. Zinszer, *Customer Service: Meaning and Measurement*, NCPDM, Chicago, 1976.

CUSTOMER DEVELOPMENT

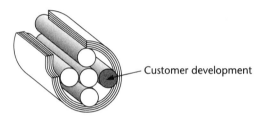

Customer development

The role of marketing is to create and keep customers.
Ted Levitt, *Marketing Imagination*

INTRODUCTION

*I*n many organizations, there is a gap between the management of customers and products. The traditional focus of brand management upon its
portfolio of products limits the company's ability to manage its portfolio of
customers on a similar basis. While sales departments may be introducing
account management systems for key customers, they are rarely aligned
with the channel objectives that marketing has for its core product brands.
Sales are often driven primarily by short-term targets and immediate transactions. Customer service departments are usually managed as a cost and
operational center – and finance views customers as debtors! The traditional
functional structure within organizations does not facilitate customer development.

With this shift away from functional hierarchies toward flat structures
and process management, customer development is emerging as a core
process. However, without reference to the UOVP marketing mix, and managing the organization's product brand and customer portfolio in particular,
the implementation of customer development strategies will lack strategic
focus.

The function of the customer development process is to build relationships
with preferred customers who favor the organization's products and services.
For each relationship to be of value to
the customer, it should be managed
from a detailed knowledge of customer
motivations, purchasing styles and purchasing strategies.

> **With the shift away from
> functional hierarchies toward
> flat structures and process
> management, customer
> development is emerging as a
> core process**

Building on the premise that all customers are not created equal, we offer
insights on how companies can manage
the customer development process more effectively by seeking to brand the
relationship with customers at the organization level. The UOVP is a more

relevant management tool for branding such relationships and the interrelationship of the UOVP with the customer development process is summarized at the end of the chapter.

Next, we argue in favor of customer loyalty and retention as a priority for customer development since it supports profitable growth by encouraging existing customers to spend more with the organization than its competitors.

THE PROFIT IMPACT OF CUSTOMER RETENTION

Ted Levitt was one of the first management gurus to recognize the importance of customer retention in the early 1980s. Since then, it has become the mantra of management consultants and business school professors on both sides of the Atlantic. However, senior management has been slower to adopt the principles of relationship management and to develop customer retention strategies. The espoused wisdom that "new is sexy, existing is boring" still dominates thinking in many boardrooms with rewards, bonuses and incentives designed to perpetuate the quest for new customers. Of course it is not wrong to seek new business with new customers but it should not be done at the expense of existing customers. So, the customer development process is a question of balance in assigning priorities to marketing and selling budgets, resources and return on investments across new and existing customers. In a recent analysis of a financial service company, budgeting priorities were heavily weighted toward new customer acquisition at the expense of cross-selling and customer retention. Upon further analysis, the company found that less than 50 percent of its nationwide customer base was profitable and the 15 percent or so of customers that were very profitable had been loyal customers over many years. The logic of the argument for developing customer retention strategies is pretty compelling and, in many ways,

counter-intuitive: differentially reward the desired behaviors of existing customers.

The work by Reichheld and Sasser (see Fig. 8.1) shows the effects of
a 5 percent increase in customer retention on profit across a number
of industry sectors.

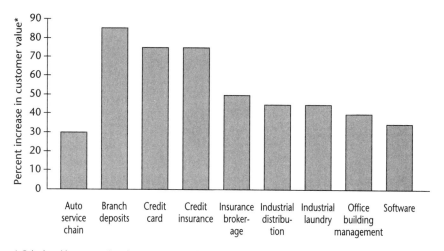

* Calculated by comparing the net present values of the profit streams for the average customer
life at current defection rates with the net present values of the profit streams for the average
customer life at 5% lower defection rates.

Source: Based on Reichheld, F.F. and Sasser, W.E. Jr, "Zero Defections: Quality Comes to Services,"
Harvard Business Review, September–October 1990, pp 105–111

**Fig. 8.1 Impact of a five-percentage point increase in retention rate
on customer net present value**

VP of Information Management at American Express, James van der
Putten, expresses the same sentiment when he refers to customer
spend: "The best customers outspend the others by ratios of 16 to 1 in
retailing, 13 to 1 in the restaurant business, 12 to 1 in airlines and 5
to 1 in the hotel/motel business."

The strategic question then becomes one of building market share
through customer acquisition and customer retention by seeking to

increase "share of customer" spend. UK grocery retailers are currently engaged in such a battle for market share and superior profits. In the past, the battleground has been for market share gains through new customers switching from more vulnerable competitors. Both Tesco and Sainsbury's have more than doubled their market shares within the last 15 years as a result. Today, they are also competing for share of customer spend (see Fig. 8.2) to grow market share as market saturation is reached.

The customer development strategies needed to build share of customer spend are fundamentally different to those of customer acquisition. The Tesco Clubcard, the chosen mechanism for reward based upon consumer spend, has directly contributed to Tesco's market share gain by lifting existing customer spend by over 13 percent. Since these retailers share nearly half the same customers (Fig. 8.2), this has

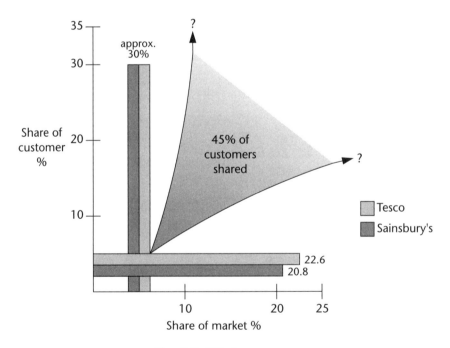

Fig. 8.2 UK store wars

led to a corresponding reduction in average spend at Sainsbury's and a consequential profit reduction for the first time in over 20 years.

How should companies go about managing customers more effectively and developing customer retention strategies? At a recent conference on relationship marketing at the Cranfield School of Management in the UK, Richard Hodapp of Managing Process Inc. reiterated the need to engage in the customer's purchase decision-making process as well as providing him with better products and services. This shift in management emphasis can lead to dramatic gains as both are germane to building customer loyalty.

> *The customer development strategies needed to build share of customer spend are fundamentally different to those of customer acquisition*

While management endeavors to increase product/service content, which undoubtedly can lead to market share gain, this is likely to produce only incremental gains with existing technologies, people and processes. In Fig. 8.3, this is termed product development strategy. However, shifts in knowledge and involvement with customer purchasing processes (customer development strategy in Fig. 8.3) can lead to more significant gains since insights developed from an early understanding of what the scope of the purchase decision is and where they are in their decision-making process can be instrumental in favorably influencing the purchase outcome. What is more, such involvement is invisible to competitors and leads to product and service developments which fit more closely with customers' emerging needs.

Customer development is relevant in business-to-business, service, and consumer markets. While the process may differ for each, they can all lead to product and customer differentiation through the most effective alignment of the organization's resources and skills base. Across all of these markets, marketing and sales management need to develop more appropriate models for mapping their customer decision processes in an attempt to establish a unified process between the

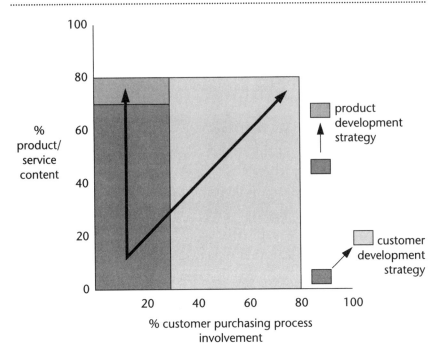

Fig. 8.3 Product content vs customer purchasing process involvement

organization and its customers. Such a unified approach is at the centre of customer loyalty management and mass customization. By
implementing customer development strategies based upon loyalty
management, high-net-worth customers can be managed so that they
benefit from a customized offer from the organization at some level.
The principles of loyalty management and the tools for customer differentiation now follow.

PRINCIPLES OF LOYALTY MANAGEMENT

There are three guiding principles to loyalty management which
strongly influence the customer development process.

Most customers buy on a portfolio basis

Loyalty is relative. In consumer markets over 95 percent of gasoline purchasers buy more than one brand, about 85 percent of customers shop at more than one grocery retailer and personal investors will on average subscribe to three different financial services. The same principle applies in business-to-business markets. The Canadian Company DiverseyLever has a leading market share in the provision of systems cleaning services in the plants of multinational food companies around the world. Currently, its global customers have different suppliers on a country basis, on a plant-by-plant basis, and within each plant. Many of these plants require up to 14 different cleaning procedures, so the challenge to management in DiverseyLever is to win more "share of plant" spend from existing customers, both within the plant and on a plant-by-plant basis. Both DiverseyLever and its customers recognize the advantages in pushing toward a unified cleaning solution. However, in order to become this preferred supplier, DiverseyLever Marketing and Sales Management has recognized the need to integrate the branding of their elements (products, service and equipment), systems (applications) and programs (expertise, applications and elements) to simplify their offer and to provide a better fit with their customers' outsourcing requirements.

All customers are not created equal

This principle has already been well established in the book. Nonetheless, the theme of profitable customers, based upon their lifetime value and supported by a relationship management approach, bears repeating. In Fig. 8.4, Bain and Company gives an account of why loyal customers are more profitable.

Their profitability stems from various cost savings within the organization, due to more effective customer service, and from the fact

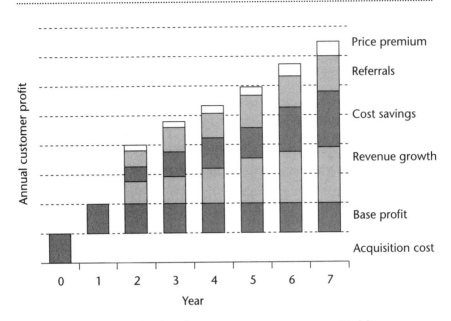

Fig. 8.4 Why loyal customers are more profitable

that loyal customers tend to devote more of their spend to preferred organizations and can act as a referral source for new customers. Reiterating a point made earlier: these profit streams flow from a relatively small number of customers. In the financial services, it is not unusual for customer analysis to reveal that 50 percent (and sometimes up to 85 percent) of an organization's profits come from the top 10 percent or 20 percent of their customers. Heinz, the consumer goods company, acknowledges that in the UK about 40 percent of its net income comes from under 5 million households. In fact, core profits are generated from something less than half this number of homes.

Loyalty is retention with attitude

It may come as something of a rude shock for customer development managers to realize that not all their customers are as involved with their products and services as they are. Car companies fret over the fact that even if the owner is satisfied with his current model, the chances are he will still buy another brand next time round. Financial services marketers used to joke that their customers were more likely to get divorced than change bank accounts. That joke has now fallen rather flat.

It is this final principle which is the key to unlock customer development and provides the mission for process management; customer development must capitalize on customer involvement where present and exploit customer indifference when it is profitable to do so. This implies segmenting markets based upon preferences in purchasing behaviors as well as psychological evaluations. For instance, if a customer spends more on a particular product than its competitors over time and is more involved with the brand in some way, these preferences suggest that brand loyalty exists. Most markets can be segmented using this simple premise and customers, or groups of customers, categorized by levels of loyalty according to their attitudes and motivations, purchasing styles and purchasing strategies.

Our research across consumer and business markets suggests that an organization's existing customer base can usually be divided broadly into four groups, according to purchasing portfolio (i.e., number of suppliers in business markets; brands bought in consumer markets) and degree of involvement (i.e., the company or brand relationship). These four groupings are shown in the Diamond of Loyalty© (see Fig. 8.5) and have designated names based upon their motivations and purchasing behaviors.

Generally, both Loyals and Habituals are high-share customers as they purchase from a narrow portfolio. They are also usually the most profitable customers to have as both exhibit behavioral loyalty. However, they have very different purchasing styles. Loyals are involved in the purchase and seek to be involved in the relationship at some level, while Habituals are behaving routinely and are fairly indifferent in their choice. So indifferent, in fact, that theirs is a routinized purchase

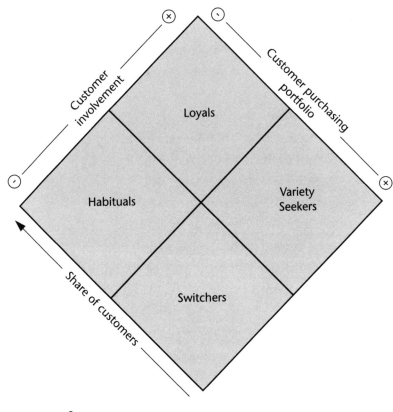

Source: Knox, Walker © 1996

Fig. 8.5 Diamond of Loyalty©: customer purchasing styles

which is dependent upon presence rather than affinity. When out-of-stocks occur or the purchase process is disrupted in other ways, switching behaviors may occur and the stream of subsequent purchases is lost until the competitor makes a similar mistake. Because of the affinity which Loyals feel toward the company or brand, switching in such circumstances is likely to be temporary until normal services are resumed. It is even possible that their purchasing decisions may be delayed – but, since loyalty is relative, it is more likely that some degree of switching by Loyals will occur.

Both Variety Seekers and Switchers exhibit similar purchasing behaviors. They buy products and services from a wide portfolio. They are low-share customers and are usually less profitable. Again, they exhibit very different purchasing motivations. For instance, Variety Seekers purchase for different usage occasions and use frequencies, according to their individual agendas. They are active in their search for brands and services (suppliers at the business level) and proactively seek multiple sourcing.

In some industry sectors, such as home improvements, the overt business strategy is based upon price being the main determinant of value

Switchers have neither affinity nor do they value presence, except on an opportunistic basis. Switchers are interested in price deals and discounts. Their purchasing strategy is to get the best deal each time purely on a transaction basis. Frederick Reichheld captures the characteristics of a Switcher beautifully in his book, *The Loyalty Effect*:

> If your business decided to scour the market place for the worst imaginable customers with the lowest coefficients of loyalty, you could hardly do better than to choose price discounts or mass distributions of coupons. Customers who glide into your arms for a minimal price discount are the same customers who dance away with someone else at the slightest enticement. Coupons and price discounts find these customers like heat-seeking missiles.

In some industry sectors, such as home improvements, the overt business strategy is based upon price being the main determinant of value. According to the CEO of one of the leading home improvement stores in the UK, customer loyalty does not exist in this market. He is quoted as saying, "If you want loyalty, buy a dog!" Research would certainly seem to support his view since three out of four customers, when questioned in-store, have difficulty remembering which of the three main home improvement stores they are currently in. Viewed from a different strategic perspective, it may be that competition based upon price incentives encourages switching behavior and provides little reason for potentially loyal customers to develop an affinity, or for latent Habituals to develop routines since they may be attracted by the competitor's most recent price incentives.

All in all, price-based competition should be avoided (unless the organization is structured for low-cost, no frills customer development) and Switchers left for the competition to attract and serve to their cost.

Of the four customer groupings described by the Diamond of Loyalty©, the behaviors of Variety Seekers are the most difficult to model both in understanding their product and services requirements and their purchasing process as each may vary considerably. To effectively serve these customers, organizations will require both a wide product range and a suitable relationship which involves them during their purchasing deliberations. Wine purchasing, typically, involves such variety-seeking purchasing behaviors and serves to illustrate the high relative cost of serving such customers.

An upmarket wine store with a number of different branches in the London area has recently carried out a loyalty-based segmentation. The management found that about two-thirds of their sales went to either Variety Seekers or to Loyals who represented less than one-third of their existing customer base. Each bought from a portfolio of brands. Typically, Variety Seekers would buy their preferred wine no more often than one bottle in 15, while Loyals would choose it about one bottle in five. To attract and retain these Loyals is a relatively straightforward customer development process: innovate through product and merchandising while building direct relationships with this customer base through customer service. The rewards would be an increased share of spend from these profitable customers.

To achieve the same effect among Variety Seekers would need the stimulation of sales promotions and a large and varied stock. Both requirements lead to a triple whammy of cost: the cost of stocking and marketing wines of marginal interest to people who shop for wine in a relatively complex and unpredictable way. Customer development would be well advised to selectively reward their Loyals and to simplify the purchasing process for their Habituals in order to grow their share of spend which is currently just under 20 percent.

The principles of loyalty management imply that effective customer development requires moving away from mass marketing, where all customers are treated as equal, and crass marketing where new customers are treated more equally than loyals. Loyalty management implies making the existing customer base a priority and assigning resources on a differentiated basis. Essentially this means that high-share customers are supported in their behaviors and beliefs with a package of benefits that befits their estimated economic worth to the organization while low-share customers receive the reverse treatment.

The notion of cutting support to low-share customers is an interesting idea from two perspectives. First, it forces marketing and management in general to ask unasked questions, such as, "What would happen if we didn't extend our usual promotion to all customers or if we insisted on prior payment from bad payers who buy from us very occasionally?" Second, it frees management and resources to concentrate on the customers who really build the business and lead to profitable growth. Both aspects of customer management are considered next in the broader context of the customer development process.

MANAGING CUSTOMER DEVELOPMENT

The UOVP serves to direct customer development toward building strong relationships with the organization's potentially most profitable customers. Marketing, in this scenario, will increasingly be based upon branding these relationships rather than solely developing the USP for individual products and services. Optimizing the portfolio of customers and product brands means making strategic choices based upon informed research into customer segment profitability and product profitability. As previously discussed, this optimization is a UOVP management activity and once it has been carried out, even on first cut basis, it should lead to the clear insights which have been uncovered in other businesses, such as:

- Product proliferation does not usually generate customer value; it can confuse through meaningless choice.
- Product proliferation shortens product lifecycles.
- The cost of such activities, in terms of developing, packaging, manufacturing and distributing marginal products before promotion is paid for by customers, particularly Loyals.
- Promotional activity rewards Switchers and teaches customers to buy deals not products.

Exactly how much market inefficiency and waste customers are paying for is hard to estimate. Paul Polman, Procter & Gamble's UK Managing Director, estimates it to be in the region of 8 percent of final selling price. In less efficient organizations, this figure could be much higher. With UOVP management commitment to auditing product brand and customer portfolios and providing guidance as to which of these products and customer groupings are mission critical, the customer development process can be more effectively managed, right down to the tails of both product brands and customers where rationalization commences.

IMPLEMENTING CUSTOMER DEVELOPMENT

Support high-share customers

At Volvo, the marketing and sales team manages customers who spend $250,000 on their cars. They are not talking about fleet buyers, but individuals buying, servicing, selling and repeat purchasing every 2.3 years over their lifetime. The figure is notional and serves to represent the lifetime value of loyal customers to the organization as a whole and the importance of "cradle to grave" customer service. Yet, only recently the company was run on a functional basis, with profit and cost centers. The marketing and selling of new cars was separated from second-hand sales, and parts and service made the real profits. Somewhere along the line, probably due to the legacy of product- or brand-management organizations, the customer fell between the cracks in the bid to shift metal out of their dealers' showrooms. They were seeking to reach the widest possible group of customers for this year's model by treating all customers as new customers, whether they were or not. Today, as data warehousing and database management become more accessible from a cost point of view, there simply is no reason why very detailed information about each car buyer should not be collected over time and high-share customers rewarded, so that they never buy another brand of car.

In a sweeping reorganization of its marketing function, American Express turned itself into a customer management organization. Each card member is now assigned into a loyalty group, such as frequent business travellers or high-value card members, so that they can be differentially rewarded according to their patterns of transactions with the company.

In business-to-business markets, key account management is a natural development of the customer development process

In business-to-business markets, key account management is a natural development of the customer development process. The strategy and structure of the management process should be based upon the expenditure and share of market of individual customers who have also been assessed against other account-specific criteria, such as growth potential, profitability and affinity. Broadly, there are three stages in this customer development process, as shown in Fig. 8.6.

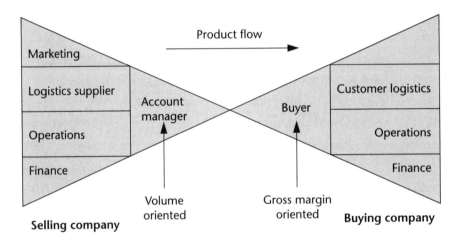

Fig. 8.6 Traditional buyer–supplier relationship

The traditional account management structure is volume- and gross margin-oriented. Although the customer warrants an account manager, relationships are essentially one to one between account manager and buyer with both having "dotted line" resources, drawn from logistics, marketing, or finance as need arises. Such boundaries between the organization and customers are fragile and can be severed relatively simply. They do not particularly nourish relationship building, trust, or share of customer growth. This traditional buyer–seller relationship corresponds to Level 1 of the partnership continuum discussed in Chapter 5 on supply partnerships. Most packaged goods companies now organize their efforts around retail chain customers in this way. Some have moved into an optimization phase so that supply chain objectives can be more closely aligned. Figure 8.7 illustrates the structure typical of such relationships.

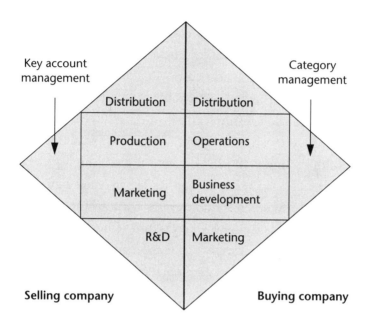

Fig. 8.7 Optimizing the buyer–supplier relationship

Instead of the manufacturer simply considering consumer loyalty to their products, such partnerships with retailers enable a common goal of shopper loyalty to both store and brand portfolios. This goal requires a large leap in faith for both parties since the logic may mean dramatic changes in brand portfolios, space allocation, measurement systems, and organizational structures. The whole point of category optimization, or category management, is to go into it without preconceptions. As one Coca-Cola executive remarked, "You let the process guide you to the outcome. So in this context, your brands have to take care of themselves." This category management approach corresponded to Level 2 in the partnership continuum of Chapter 5.

The third phase of account management is the seamless organization, illustrated in Fig. 8.8. In effect, "Our people are your people" becomes the philosophical and managerial end point through quasi-integration. Costing systems become transparent. Joint research and development takes place and there are interfaces at every level and function between the organizations. Information systems integration is utilized to reduce transaction costs. The Procter & Gamble – Wal-Mart relationship in the USA is probably the best known example of such a synergistic relationship. Currently, over 100 P&G people work full time in Wal-Mart's head office in Bentonville, Arkansas. The P&G team is multifunctional and its role is to provide supply chain integration and leadership across categories led by their brands and to take cost out of the replenishment cycle. Without the highest levels of transparency and trust between companies, they would be ineffectual in striving for a total supply chain approach to value creation for their consumers. Such relationships correspond to Level 3 in the partnership continuum (Chapter 5).

The logic of building your business through a customer development process which supports growth in share of spend across the right customers has a resonant ring. Not only does this lead to increased profitability, but these customers also generate a positive cashflow which may be reinvested in the organization's people, processes and product development to further increase fit and sustain continued loyalty. By the same token, bad interactions with customers can lead to negative cashflow, reduced profitability and general hassle.

Let go of low-share customers

A corollary to differentiating your high-share customers is identifying

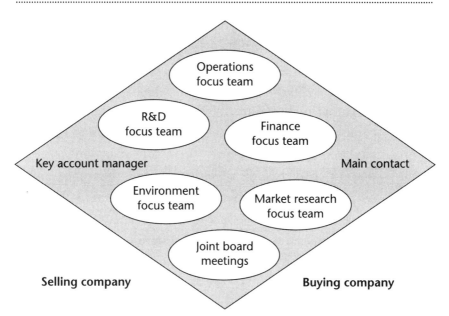

Source: M. McDonald and B. Rogers, Cranfield School of Management, 1996

Fig. 8.8 The seamless organization

and trimming the tail of low-share customers. Most companies do not face up to the prospect of letting such customers go. In this book, we are suggesting that such surgery is really restricted to out-and-out Switchers. They are not committed to either the organization or its products and they purchase from a wide portfolio of competitive suppliers. Since they shop around, their share of spend on any preferred supplier is low and there is little prospect of profitably altering these behaviors. Most management involved in customer development can readily identify the 5 to 10 percent of customers who fall into this extreme category. Once identified, they can be selectively rationalized and resources redirected toward building more profitable relationships.

Media advertising is a particular case in point where more resource is focused on non-purchasers than purchasers in building customer relationships! It was Lord Leverhulme who once said in the 1920s, "I know that half my advertising is wasted, the problem is I don't know which half." In the 1990s, with media fragmentation and cost inflation eroding declining advertising budgets, it could be argued that perhaps as much as four-fifths of advertising spend is now wasted. Broadly, this is because media planners cannot readily identify the 20 percent or so of high-share customers who purchase around 80 percent of brand volume. Consequently, these consumers only receive about 20 percent of the brand's advertising impressions since advertising spend correlates with segment size. The remaining 80 percent of advertising impressions are spread across consumers who are medium-to-light buyers, those who are disinterested and, worst still, the very large number who do not even buy from the category. To reverse this effect requires a new way of thinking about media planning and expenditure goals on a product-by-product basis and at the organization level, since consumers will buy from a portfolio of the organization's brands with varying degrees of involvement.

UOVP and the customer development process

The customer development process is directed by each of the UOVP marketing mix elements. For instance, reputation goes beyond product brands and services and strikes at the heart of the organization's values and capabilities which shape the purchasing experiences of customers. These purchase experiences, whether based upon customized solutions from a wide network of the organization's relationships or the consumption of a standard product, determine levels of customer affinity and involvement. It is these preferences which form the tools for customer differentiation and development.

Performance benchmarking depends upon monitoring customer satisfactions and measuring key performance indicators of products and services that feed back continuously into the customer development process. With regard to product brand and customer portfolio, we stressed earlier that customer relationships cannot now be considered merely as a byproduct of the sales of individual products or services. Nor can these products be evaluated solely by their net present value (NPV). The customer relationship is based upon the estimated lifetime value of each customer across the organization's brand portfolio.

Equally, serving the right customers with the appropriate brand and services portfolio can lead to increased leverage in the value chain and opportunities for new relationships with suppliers and alliances. So, there is also a reverse effect which needs to be acknowledged between process and UOVP activities. This interrelationship with customer development determines levels of customer intimacy and the extent of customization. It should also determine the appropriate balance between customer acquisition and retention as each have differing customer development requirements.

Without successful customer development, alignment of the other customer-facing processes becomes more difficult. However, without UOVP strategy to provide the blueprint for process implementation, alignment will be lacking and implementation largely process directed.

SUMMARY

As process management fast becomes recognized as the means by which customer value can be created, it is now equally well understood that the mechanism of value delivery is along the core processes. Without managing the customer development process, the implementation of strategic plans will lack clear focus. We argue that the function of the customer development process is to build relationships with preferred customers. Working on the premise that all customers are not created equal, the priority for

customer development in mature markets is to build these preferred relationships among existing customers in order to increase
their share of spend over time. It is now accepted wisdom that
these customer relationships deliver superior profits. How customer development management select these customers, or
groups of customers, and build specific relationships is directed by
the principles of loyalty management.

These principles acknowledge that customer loyalty is relative
which means that customers as well as product and service brands
need to be differentiated. The Diamond of Loyalty© provides a
new management tool for this purpose by categorizing customer
purchasing styles according to their level of involvement (i.e.,
brand or company relationship) and their purchasing portfolio
across suppliers.

Optimizing the portfolio of customers and product brands
means making strategic choices informed by marketing research.
Clearly, marketing management is in a strong position to provide
this leadership and ultimately to direct the customer development process as the UOVP architecture is fashioned.

Management of the customer development process falls to an
integrated marketing and sales team. At the strategic level of
building and branding customer relationships, marketing should
be assessing resource priorities among product and service brands
and across customer groups. Sales management should then align
its key account selling and customer support services to fit the
level of priority designated to each customer group.

Successful implementation means adapting these structures as
customer relationships change. Since these relationships are
dynamic by nature, adaptations should be made to support the
purchasing behaviors of high-share customers while low-share
customers become candidates for review and possible rationalization. In particular, this applies to the group of customers catego-

rized as Switchers as the relationship tends to be transactional both at a product brand and an organization level.

The customer development process is strongly influenced by UOVP management of the product brand and customer portfolio. However, it is also conditioned by the other UOVP mix variables since the organization's reputation, its product and service performance and its ability to manage alliances are continuously assessed by customers who also make decisions about relationships at the product brand and organization level.

Further reading

There is a number of books and reports supporting the arguments presented in this chapter. First among these is Frederick Reichheld's book, *The Loyalty Effect*. He provides extensive research drawn from Bain & Co into the profit impact of customer loyalty and retention.

- Frederick Reichheld, *The Loyalty Effect*, Harvard Business School Press, Boston, MA, 1996.

Don Peppers and Martha Rogers, in their books *The One to One Future* and *Enterprise One to One*, explore the transition from mass marketing to customer-of-one thinking. The orientation of these books is very much about developing customer relationships for long-term profit streams.

- Don Peppers and Martha Rogers, *The One to One Future*, Doubleday, New York, 1993.

- Don Peppers and Martha Rogers, *Enterprise One to One*, Doubleday, New York, 1997.

Garth Hallberg's book on consumer purchasing behavior and the management of consumer brands makes the case for supporting desired behaviors through the application of the Pareto Principle to fast moving consumer goods (f.m.c.g.) marketing. He stresses the profit contribution made by a small percentage of purchasers in consumer goods markets.

- Garth Hallberg, *All Consumers are not Created Equal*, John Wiley, New York, 1995.

For a visionary discussion of the future role of marketing, Ted Levitt's *The Marketing Imagination* is an influential book.

- Ted Levitt, *The Marketing Imagination*, Collier-Macmillan, London, 1983.

- Malcolm McDonald, Tony Millman and Beth Rogers, "Key Account Management: Learning from Supplier and Customer Perspectives," Cranfield School of Management Publication, Cranfield, 1996.

- Simon Knox and David Walker, "New Empirical Perspectives on Brand Loyalty: Implications for Segmentation Strategy and Equity," in D. Arnott *et al.* (eds), *Proceedings on Marketing: Progress, Prospects and Perspectives*, vol. 2, pp 1313–1328, Warwick, 1997.

- Simon Knox and Tim Denison, "Exploring Shopping Behaviour amongst Primary Shoppers: Patterns in Store Loyalty and Expenditure," J. Bloemer *et al.* (eds), *Proceedings on Marketing: its Dynamics and Challenges*, pp 167–186, Maastricht, 1994.

MEASURING THE VALUE GAP

INTRODUCTION: ARE YOU IN THE RIGHT RACE?

W*e have outlined our premise that traditional marketing theory is no longer sufficient to guide the company's customer value strategies. It is predicated upon a basic assumption, explicit or implicit, that customer value arises largely from the exchange of goods and services. This premise has been developed into an extensive theory of marketing and brand-based competition. For years, marketing management have been obsessed with the creation of brand value as it is felt that brands are the last line of defense against lower cost imitators.*

Over the past decade we have witnessed a divergence between the activities that create brand value (the 4Ps) and those that create customer value. The new business mantra of "listen and serve" is the guideline for creating customer value today and it demands a radically new approach to marketing and brand strategy, namely:

- *The organization brand, the UOVP, is the best facilitator of productive relationships with individual customers.*
- *Business processes must be turned to face and serve individual customers from end to end, running across the old functional stovepipes.*
- *Processes must be fused with the company's UOVP to ensure that process improvement remains a means to an end (creating a better and differentiated proposition to customers), rather than the end itself.*

> **The new business mantra of "listen and serve" is the guideline for creating customer value today**

- *Marketing management no longer form the start of a sequential process that determines innovation and customer needs. They must evolve into business systems integrators who work much more interactively throughout the value chain.*

If this argument is intuitively appealing to the reader, then the following questions spring to mind:

- *How do I know the extent of the value gap in my organization and in my industry?*
- *How much larger (smaller) is this gap compared to my competitors?*
- *What are the key determinants of the value gap that affect my organization?*
- *What is the first step to be taken to close this value gap?*

This chapter provides a limited diagnostic tool which managers can use to shed light on these questions.

THE DIAGNOSTIC

Introduction

The diagnostic consists of three separate questionnaires that address the key steps in creating the UOVP, namely, the extent to which your organization:

1 Creates customer value that is unique and identifiable.
2 Has developed its end-to-end business processes from the customer through the supply chain.
3 Integrates these business process with its unique, identifiable customer value proposition.

In each of these questionnaires, you are asked to rate relevant attributes or statements on a five-point scale; the summation of the individual question scores provides an overall score for that step of UOVP development. These scores allow you to place your organization on a continuum which characterizes this step. The step 1 continuum contrasts product-centered against customer-centered value delivery, step 2 looks at functionally managed structures against process managed and step 3 at the level of integration between process and proposition.

Scores that place your organization in the middle of these continua are interpreted as meaning that your organization is in transition toward the new approach both to marketing and value creation that we have identified earlier. This methodology, therefore, assumes that the UOVP is the desired end goal.

Using the diagnostic effectively

We have no doubt that readers will appreciate the obvious limitations of such a "do-it-yourself" tool. While we hope that it acts as a catalyst for valuable internal and external discussion, the methodology of selecting your customer value proposition and integrating your core business processes requires a far more rigorous analysis.

That said, our experience of using simple questionnaires in companies demonstrates that they can be a powerful tool for getting disagreements out into the open, allowing the top team to agree on the dimensions of the problems that they face and the language they wish to use in moving forward. We have found it particularly useful when companies invite participation across their own business units or from different layers in the supply chain. Matched questionnaires concerning the company's value proposition across business units or functional groups can expose serious rifts and historic compromises that are holding the organization back. A similar exercise that involves supply partners and customers has often proven to be a poignant "reality check," revealing gaps between how others see us and how we see ourselves.

Naturally, you might consider modifying the diagnostic to precisely reflect your own organization's situation.

Step 1: Creating unique customer value

In Table 9.1 there are seven questions concerning customer value. Against each question, check the box which you think best describes

Table 9.1 Unique customer value questionnaire

Against each question, check one box on the right according to how strongly you agree or disagree

	disagree strongly	disagree	neither agree nor disagree	agree	agree strongly
1 Our customers would agree that, more so than our competitors, we go out of our way to understand what value means to them.	1 ☐	2 ☐	3 ☐	4 ☐	5 ☐
2 Our new product (service) introduction success rate is better than our competitors because it has been carefully developed with this customer value in mind.	1 ☐	2 ☐	3 ☐	4 ☐	5 ☐
3 Our customers appreciate that we keep a close monitor of our relationships with them at all levels in our organization across the range of product/service brands they purchase.	1 ☐	2 ☐	3 ☐	4 ☐	5 ☐
4 Our customers appreciate that our business processes are integrated with theirs and feel that our competencies are also available to them.	1 ☐	2 ☐	3 ☐	4 ☐	5 ☐
5 Customers perceive that our ability to mobilize these company competencies in their service is better than our competitors.	1 ☐	2 ☐	3 ☐	4 ☐	5 ☐
6 We play a leading role in shaping the supply chain in which we operate and our role is appreciated by customers and suppliers.	1 ☐	2 ☐	3 ☐	4 ☐	5 ☐
7 We don't often lose customers to competitors that position themselves as offering a better total package of benefits. Our own competencies and those of our partners are fully competitive.	1 ☐	2 ☐	3 ☐	4 ☐	5 ☐

your organization's approach to creating customer value. As you do, however, make sure you consider your response relative to your competition since your customers are likely to view your endeavors in this light.

How does your organization score? Add up your scores for the seven questions (disagree strongly = 1, disagree = 2, etc.) and place your organization on the customer value continuum based upon your total score (Fig. 9.1).

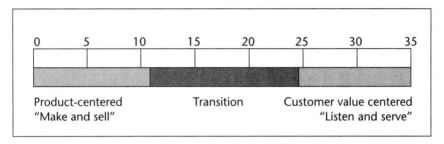

Fig. 9.1 Customer value continuum

Customer value centered

The further to right of 25 points, the more likely it is that your organization is truly focused on creating customer value and not merely product brand value. Your responses suggest that the business is very customer focused and that you are a leading player in an extended network of suppliers and partners structured to build customer value. Your customers probably see you as a valued partner and look to your resources in order to help them achieve their business goals. They value you for your ability to lead and integrate complex supply chains and networks of alliances in their service. You likely share confidential information about each others' long-term goals and objectives. This provides you with an organization proposition that your competitors find hard to imitate as it is broadly based throughout the organization in a service culture with unique competencies and a real partnership attitude. In short, you are in a relationship with customers to deliver a stream of value over time and help your customers achieve their ambitions by "listening and serving."

Product-centered

A score under 12, however, implies that the organization is inflexible and inwardly focused; it does not actively solicit, nor react to customer feedback. There is very little understanding of the issues that matter to the client and the organization is vulnerable to competing supply chains offering a much more attractive solution. It does not seek to integrate its business processes with those of its customers. In our experience, the perceived wisdom in such organizations is that its customers do not want partners, they merely take whatever you offer and ask for more at the next negotiation: "What really matters to our customers is price, price and price!" Of course, one might ask what else you have offered them. A low score on this questionnaire is an indication that what really matters to the organization is the manufacture of standardized products and services. You are still living in a "make and sell" world.

Transition

Many organizations will score in between the two extremes; this is perhaps a better approximation of reality. Most organizations have become more effective in the past decade through management improvements. Consequently, they have moved at least some way toward being customer value driven. The issue for those who find themselves in the transition part of the continuum is to identify the obstacles that block improvements and to find a way forward. Organizations in transition have most likely embarked upon a number of process improvement programs and achieved a good measure of success. However, a medium score on this diagnostic indicates that the programs have not been fully effective. It may be that:

1   The organization has become much more customer value centered in recent years but retains a functional structure which is no longer sufficiently flexible and reactive to achieve breakthroughs in creating new customer value.

2   The organization has traditionally been product-centered but has introduced some level of process management to increase flexibility and remove cost. Here, the management is trying to hold on to both ends, since the old is more comfortable while the new is relatively untested. This has introduced conflict and tension through the organization. Cost savings have been realized and these have been passed on to the customer, but the organization does not feel like a world-beater.

We would argue that both situations are insupportable in the long term. However, organizations in transition can survive in the short term because customer value is understood at some level within the company. The challenge to management within either type of organization is to unite their value creating activities with their value-delivery steps which are the core processes. In UOVP terms, both need to be managed as an integrated whole through the cycle of value research, development and management.

Step 2: Developing end-to-end processes

In this diagnostic step, you should be able to gauge the level to which your organization has adjusted to process-management thinking. If this reengineering has not yet occurred and you consider your organization to have a predominantly functional structure, you can see just how peripheral your core processes are to your marketplace strategy.

For those unfamiliar with process-based techniques, or merely confused by the plethora of terminology surrounding this area, the five processes that we have identified will suffice for the purpose of this diagnostic.

Table 9.2 Representative business processes

Supply partnership	Asset management	Resource transformation	Customer development	Marketing planning
Integrated logistics	Brand management	JIT	Key account management	Segmentation
JIT	Training	Kanban	Relationship marketing	Competitive benchmarking
Vendor-managed inventory	Added value analysis (AVA)	Time to market	Loyalty management	Portfolio analysis
Supply chain management	Flexible manufacturing	New product development	Customer service	Market selection
		Total quality	Efficient consumer response (ECR)	Process mapping
		Cycle time reduction		

Of course, process consultants and corporate change agents may wish to introduce their own terminology in this area. We do not see this as a problem; language is a powerful agent of change and it can be used to suit individual company programs. Table 9.2 places some representative business processes and management techniques in the context of the five core processes we have discussed in Chapters 4 to 8.

Whatever labels management wishes to attach to processes, most experienced consultants in the field suggest that organizations have a relatively small set of core processes that produce key results. These processes undoubtedly do exist in your organization and, if they are

> *Most experienced consultants in the field suggest that organizations have a relatively small set of core processes that produce key results*

not readily identifiable, it may simply mean that your management structure has not been reconfigured around them.

Base your judgment on the processes that you can identify as creating the most value for customers. Once you have in mind what these core processes are, fill in the process development questionnaire (Table 9.3).

How does your organization score?

Functionally managed

A low score in this part of the diagnostic (Fig. 9.2) indicates an organization whose approach to customers is driven by a traditional or functional approach to working. Information is sequentially processed through individual departments and through supply chain partners. Decision making is slow and uninformed; everyone is looking to optimize only a small part of the total solution. This series of information hand-offs actually serves to distance the customer from the organization. It may feel as if you are living in an unreal world that is more self-serving than customer serving. Senior management is frustrated by the lack of bold initiatives coming up from the

Table 9.3 Process development questionnaire

Against each question, check one box on the right according to how strongly you agree or disagree

	disagree strongly	disagree	neither agree nor disagree	agree	agree strongly
1 We are rigorous in identifying the business processes that add the greatest amounts of customer value. Our core processes are not simply existing functional units relabeled.	1 ☐	2 ☐	3 ☐	4 ☐	5 ☐
2 There are key measures by which each core process is assessed. These are created from a customer perspective and we benchmark our achievements versus competitors and best-in-class.	1 ☐	2 ☐	3 ☐	4 ☐	5 ☐
3 Our organization is structured to manage these core processes and to continually improve them.	1 ☐	2 ☐	3 ☐	4 ☐	5 ☐
4 Customers and suppliers play a full part in directing our core processes and help us improve them. We work with them to determine what is important; there is a high degree of trust and sharing through the supply chain.	1 ☐	2 ☐	3 ☐	4 ☐	5 ☐
5 Customer feedback is not handed off through the organization, department by department, to our suppliers and all the way back through the loop to customers. We work in "real time," sharing information through the chain.	1 ☐	2 ☐	3 ☐	4 ☐	5 ☐
6 The organization has the information needed to make each core process completely visible, end to end. This information is available to frontline staff in a timely and easily understood manner.	1 ☐	2 ☐	3 ☐	4 ☐	5 ☐
7 It is common practice for our process owners to play a major role in the creation of business plans and in decisions about resource allocation. Investment in process development is not merely a byproduct of individual product or business unit plans.	1 ☐	2 ☐	3 ☐	4 ☐	5 ☐

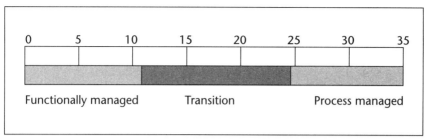

Fig. 9.2 Process development continuum

organization, junior managers are frustrated by the time and effort required for the smallest of initiatives and middle managers feel besieged from all sides.

Process managed

If your score places your organization in the process-managed sector of the continuum, we believe that it is likely that the feel of your organization is the antithesis of the functional structure described earlier. People feel close to the customer and can see how their individual efforts fit into an overall picture. Problems and opportunities are rapidly identified from all parts of the supply chain and teams form to quickly address them. The pace of work may seem frenetic, but there is a real feeling of progress and moving forward. The key characteristic of the people in the organization is helpful and responsive. Their network of colleagues extends through the supply chain and they probably would find it easier to work for the customer, or the supplier, than for the competition.

Process development is well advanced and supply chain relationships are extensive. The question then becomes how well are these processes integrated to deliver a unique customer value proposition? This is addressed in step 3 of our diagnostic.

Transition

By definition, the transition portion of the continuum is a bit of both.

Process management has likely been agreed to by senior management and under implementation. The journey from function to process is known to progress slowly with occasional detours.

Following a large scale study of reengineering success and failures in Europe and North America, CSC advised reengineers to be selective, plan better, and shoot higher. The key success factors in moving from functional to process-based management were identified as high ambition, senior management commitment and effective program management.

> **The journey from function to process is known to progress slowly with occasional detours**

Step 3: Integrating the customer value proposition with processes

The last step of the diagnostic is to determine the extent to which the customer value (measured in step 1) and business processes (step 2) work together. It is intuitively appealing and there is research to support the idea that aligning the customer value proposition to the organization's internal workings leads to better business performance. The point of process management is not to produce "quality" goods and services that customers do not wish to buy, nor is it the objective of those creating the customer offer to "sell" that which cannot be delivered.

The final questionnaire explores the extent to which your business is driven to integrated customer value and process delivery. Work through the seven questions in Table 9.4 by checking the box which best describes your integration procedures.

As before, add up your scores to arrive at your total out of 35.

If your score is toward the higher end of the integration continuum, it suggests that your processes are determined by both customer value and the resources required to create and deliver that value. If your

Table 9.4 Value and process integration

Against each question, check one box on the right according to how strongly you agree or disagree

	disagree strongly	disagree	neither agree nor disagree	agree	agree strongly
1 We periodically undertake a very broad review of customer value drivers. Key process owners participate fully in this activity.	1 ☐	2 ☐	3 ☐	4 ☐	5 ☐
2 Process owners are empowered to lead organizational change on the basis of customer feedback.	1 ☐	2 ☐	3 ☐	4 ☐	5 ☐
3 Investments and process improvement programs are planned in line with the organization's value proposition.	1 ☐	2 ☐	3 ☐	4 ☐	5 ☐
4 Investment in our assets, competencies and processes are driven by measures of customer value more than cost.	1 ☐	2 ☐	3 ☐	4 ☐	5 ☐
5 Customers regularly make use of our assets in expanding their business. Our competencies are a vital component of their overall success.	1 ☐	2 ☐	3 ☐	4 ☐	5 ☐
6 Our people are aware of their contribution to customer value and make their daily decisions on that basis.	1 ☐	2 ☐	3 ☐	4 ☐	5 ☐
7 We lead, rather than follow.	1 ☐	2 ☐	3 ☐	4 ☐	5 ☐

assessment is toward the 5–10 point end of the scale, then greater alignment is needed and the UOVP procedures may prove useful in determining the direction of this alignment.

Mid-scores imply that you are managing customer value creation and business process development well, but separately. Both are necessary when determining priorities and leading networks that deliver customer value. This is why, in Chapter 4, we place UOVP marketing planning as the central wire in our cable and wires model. Without this process of systematically reviewing the value determinants and process efficiencies, customer relationships developed through product and service brands will remain rather two-dimensional.

Diagnostic summary

There are three steps to our diagnosis and each offers three positions on a continuum giving 27 possible solutions. It is not our intention to take the reader through each solution in this chapter. However, there are some obvious patterns that emerge. The four patterns we normally observe are:

1   We would predict that if your scores indicate that your organization strongly aligns its customer value approach with its key processes, it will be successful and increasingly valued by your customers.

2   Companies that are product-centered and functionally-oriented will have increasing difficulty in generating sufficient levels of customer value, regardless of the extent to which they can align processes with proposition.

3   Product-centered organizations, even those that have embraced process management, will hit limitations in the potential of their product brands to create value. They may be feeling that process-based management has not delivered as promised, but the problem may lie more in the extent to which their products are able to generate customer value in the modern economy.

4   Finally, there are those companies that have embraced process management almost at the exclusion of marketplace strategy. They may find that while their performance indicators are moving up, the market is moving away from them because their process management is out of alignment with customer value. Thus, process

development may be well advanced but value alignment has yet to be managed effectively.

UOVP revisited

Although our three-step diagnostic contains only 21 sample questions, it should raise some of the key issues that a more thorough and systematic audit would undoubtedly uncover. It should also indicate the extent to which the practices of marketing must change in order to return to its value-creating roots. There are no clever short cuts or silver bullets in the UOVP model; rather, a lot of hard work by everyone in the organization to create and manage business systems that add real customer value.

The UOVP provides an architecture for such a transformation. Because the starting point and the UOVP mix is different for each organization, we cannot offer a stage-by-stage route map to structural change. The nature of the transformation is potentially so large that such a prescription is neither credible nor desirable.

In the final chapter of our book, we challenge conventional marketing orthodoxies and structures by highlighting the new basic assumptions for the rehabilitation of marketing and for the UOVP methodology to be successfully implemented.

SUMMARY

This chapter offers a simplified diagnostic tool that covers the three key steps of UOVP architecture: differentiated customer value proposition, end-to-end business process development and the integration of UOVP brand proposition with process so that these processes are directed to support customer value.

Using the three-step diagnostic questionnaires, companies can be scored on a continuum at each step leading to the UOVP architecture.

Those companies which are consistently scoring around the mid-points on each continuum are considered to be in transition to UOVP management. They have likely begun a number of process-based change programs but have yet to "come through at the other end." Their challenge is to identify obstacles to further improvements which is where the UOVP can be very useful in enabling this to happen. Companies with low scores are in danger of being marginalized without instigating major changes in process management and value determination. Finally, companies with high scores would suggest that process and proposition are aligned and their change programs are creating real value for their customers.

THE REHABILITATION
OF MARKETING

INTRODUCTION

We have made the case that the traditional thinking and practices of marketing alone, in particular the management of product brands, are insufficient to manage the transition brand marketing has entered. Too little of what marketing does fundamentally addresses the issues of what customer value is and how the organization can interpret this in determining its proposition to the market. Without a continuous focus on this alignment of brand with customer value, marketing risks becoming a self-indulgence.

> **Without a continuous focus on the alignment of brand with customer value, marketing risks becoming a self-indulgence**

Throughout this book, we have attempted to explain how the UOVP – Unique Organisation Value Proposition™ – provides the methodology for bridging this value gap by aligning value-producing business processes to a differentiated customer offer. In Chapter 9, we provided a simplified diagnostic tool that can point to the existence of the value gap within your organization. If you perceive that there is a value gap, the final question remains as to who should lead the development of the UOVP.

Should it be marketing management?

At the risk of over-generalization, marketers have a number of skills and characteristics that make many well suited to becoming the architects of the UOVP. At its best, marketing develops people skilled in understanding competitive strategy, customer motivation and purchasing processes. In addition, the

> **The marketing function is often an obstacle to companies implementing rapid, large-scale change**

marketing function has traditionally attracted entrepreneurial managers capable of innovation. These talents need to be redirected from building brands for their own sake, toward developing business systems that add value to customers.

There are, of course, many marketers already doing just that by demon-strating leadership within their organizations, creating customer value and developing the business systems needed to deliver it. However, our own expe-rience, and that of many colleagues specializing in change management, suggests that the marketing function is often an obstacle to companies implementing rapid, large-scale change.

THE TRADITIONAL MARKETING FUNCTION
CAN BE PART OF THE PROBLEM

Where marketing management act as a catalyst for change, it tends to be on their terms. At its worst, marketing begins the discussion about the need for change with such expressions as "when we get serious about branding" or "when we get serious about investment." If their budget is less than their competitors, "we cannot win." If it is larger, "we need to maintain it so as to create insurmountable barriers for competitors." If the competitor extends its product portfolio, "we must respond so as not to be outflanked." If customers wish to rene-gotiate the terms of trade, "we must hold firm or we erode our brand position." In the 1980s, when the brand was king, this reasoning was indulged.

In the 1990s, colleagues are growing tired of the brand-building mantras.

The problems that marketing management must face up to include methodology, structure, process, and reward. We have explored the traditional methodologies employed by marketers – the augmented brand, the USP and the 4Ps – only to find them insufficient for the modern economy.

Equally, the notion of marketing as a functional department must be reviewed. Most of the other traditional business functions have been reengineered as processes during the 1990s. One rarely hears of manufacturing today: companies have logistics, order fulfillment or supply chain processes. Sales has been replaced by customer development. R&D has been transformed into product introduction. Many companies with which we deal have only a skeleton crew directing policy for personnel or complaints; much of the work previously done by these departments has been rolled into the business processes. Marketing as a function tends to be associated with the sequential processing of information between the market and the company which we have criticized in the resource transformation chapter. Perhaps one tends to be too harsh on one's own colleagues, but we do not feel that marketing departments have transformed themselves to the same extent as have other functional groups during the 1990s.

In the rehabilitation of marketing, one must also consider the reward systems for the profession. Salary, prominence and career advancement for most marketing professionals are based on the size of their marketing budget. The best jobs, the ones representing the pinnacle of the career ladder, have advertising budgets measured in the tens of millions of dollars. To recruit good people, one must have a big budget. These are yardsticks from an era where marketing was primarily about advertising. Where is customer value in all of this?

THE BUSINESS NEED FOR REHABILITATION

Companies must seriously question the investment they make in brand building. Where the brand is aligned with customer value, the investment will bring returns. Where it is not, companies should redirect their investment to those activities that do create customer value. For some companies, particularly those serving the mass consumer market, marketing budgets can equal their entire net profits. This represents a tremendous investment in a practice that we believe is often using the wrong methodology. We have no doubt that most multibrand companies could achieve breakthrough improvements in the effectiveness of the marketing spend through the implementation of UOVP principles.

A sequential approach to processing customer feedback through the sales and marketing departments is, we believe, costing companies dearly in terms of time-to-market, customer defection and missed opportunities. The customer must be involved with as many of the organization's core processes as possible. End-to-end process management mandates the participation of customers at one end and suppliers at the other. Neither marketing nor sales functions can act as the final arbiter on customer needs or market developments. Similarly, supplier partners must have access to all parts of the organization; purchasing cannot impose itself between supplier and company. The traditional marketing department, perversely, can act as a barrier to "marketing."

> *Marketing is too important to reside in the marketing department alone, it must live within the organization and be lived by everyone*

The marketing department can create unnecessary tensions between managers and generate low morale among marketers themselves. The slow, uninformed and sequential nature of functional management creates resentment and blame when customers defect or competitors beat them to market. The marketing department is often an uncomfortable place; it used to be said of brand managers in consumer goods companies that they had all the responsibility for their brands but none of the authority necessary to run them. This feeling of disempowerment is endemic in functional organizations. Functional departments are finding it more and more difficult to produce breakthroughs in customer value. Marketing writers have long said that marketing is too important to reside in the marketing department alone, it must live within everyone in the organization and be lived by everyone.

IS THE MARKETING DEPARTMENT NEEDED ANY MORE?

If the traditional brand no longer creates customer value and the traditional marketing function is often counterproductive, what then is the need for a marketing department?

The transformation of other traditional business functions following the reengineering trend of the 1990s provides some potential answers to this very challenging question.

Marketers can learn some valuable lessons from the experiences of manufacturing over this past decade. Manufacturing has been reborn as logistics, order fulfillment and supply chain in most progressive organizations. Leaders of these processes have abandoned their traditional focus on expensive plants and technology in favor of supply partnerships and global sourcing. Information about the components and products with which they deal is more important to the process than the physical goods themselves. Some reengineered manufacturing functions no longer make anything.

However, the amount of customer and shareholder value that they have created through successful supply chain reengineering programs is staggering. When the authors started in industry over 15 years ago, logistics was a gracious title for the tedious work of purchasing and distribution. Today logistics leaders are among the most progressive and powerful members of many boards.

Finance departments, numbering tens of thousands of people in the largest corporations, have transformed themselves from sprawling hierarchies moving mountains of paper sequentially between various departments into a limited number of streamlined processes. Progressive sales groups no longer "own" the customer internally, they facilitate and coordinate a well-planned series of relationships between their organization and the customer.

At a minimum, marketing management supply a set of functional skills that will always remain important, such as market research, packaging development, communications, promotion and competitor analysis. Access to these capabilities must be provided to the organization; a center of excellence ensures that the capability is sufficient to meet the business need.

However, that is a very minimalist view of the role of marketing management in the future. Perhaps because of our origins in marketing, the authors suggest that marketers should strive to return to the heart of adding value for their organizations. For this to be possible, it must accept the same degree of change as, for example, manufacturing. Can we not envisage a brandless brand director building powerful relationships all along the supply chain and thus creating sustainable competitive advantage and profitability? Could a marketing director with no advertising budget not still create the leading organization brand in his or her market?

We maintain that the UOVP offers the right tool for rehabilitation of marketing. It will focus investment on activities that generate customer value regardless if they are classical brand-based programs or not. It will align the company behind a clear and manageable customer proposition and involve customers and suppliers in delivering it. In so doing, a new form of brand building will take place, one that is more suited for how customer value is created today.

THE REHABILITATED MARKETING CAPABILITY

Marketing management will be rehabilitated when the organization elects it to lead the UOVP brand-building process. Marketers must now earn the right to build the UOVP and lead the new branding process, for it is no longer automatically conferred upon it by dint of job title. In order for marketers to be invited by their colleagues to build this brand, they must work with new basic assumptions and embrace a new role within the organization. These are now outlined.

The new basic assumptions

Customers redefine value in their own terms

The future is a customer-of-one. Just as mass marketing was replaced by segmentation marketing, marketing to individuals and individual organizations will soon become the norm, if it has not done so already. It is the customers who will specify value and direct the value chain to get what they want. The opportunity to individualize, add value and generally respond to customers' requirements in real time is simply a very different world to making available the standard product brand within the confines of a product catalog or supermarket shelf.

Customer value through business processes

Marketing management, we maintain, have been slow to recognize that it is through customer-facing processes that customer value is ultimately created and delivered. In the past, this has been because the functional silos and hierarchical structures have not acknowledged their importance nor could they readily contribute to their efficacy as an end-to-end activity. The development of the brand management system was an attempt to build this cross-functional purpose into product branding which was at the center of value creation in these functional structures.

> *In today's flat-structured organization, process leaders have replaced brand managers as the central force for integration of company effort and the fulfilling of future customer needs*

In today's flat-structured organization, process leaders have replaced brand managers as the central force for integration of company effort and the fulfilling of future customer needs.

As these processes become highly visible and are seen to have strategic significance, the likelihood of developing "horizontal silos" becomes a real concern. Although the processes individually may be working effectively and efficiently, the mechanisms for their alignment in the common pursuit of customer value could well be missing. Product and service brand delivery needs this alignment if full synergies are to be achieved. Traditional product and market-planning procedures are not likely to contribute significantly to this process integration step as they have been developed with products, not processes, as the center of value. Alignment and planning procedures now require both processes and products to be center stage.

Process management needs process-based planning

Both the content and context of marketing planning in a process-centered organization are entirely different to conventional planning procedures. In flat-structured organizations, process plans are needed rather than simply product plans. The interpretation of strategic goals and business objectives through a compilation of individual product plans and product profitabilities is to miss the point. Marketing planning must now direct process goals, through a sequence that determines the means of achieving these goals and identifies the risks to the organization. Process owners can use these new planning procedures to identify investments needed, capabilities required and to develop better working practices across processes. Product-centered planning alone will fail process owners.

4Ps planning is sandwiched between the higher determinants of value chain positioning and these wider applications of process development and integration. Marketing management, with their skills in planning procedures, need to acknowledge these developments and participate. Product planning then becomes relegated to a secondary, functional role.

Process-based planning directed by customer value

The procedures and practices of such planning must be developed through a clear understanding of what customer value is and how the organization chooses to interpret this in determining its UOVP brand architecture and process priorities. Much has been made of this theme throughout the book as we see it as being perhaps the most critical aspect of new branding; it is the bridging mechanism for reinterpreting brand and customer value across the organization.

Without the mechanism for continuous alignment, brand value ceases to be the embodiment of customer value which is why we question most if not all of the conventional orthodoxies of brand management.

Customer value and brand value continuously aligned

Marketers have been trained to act as the value creators because of their knowledge of 4Ps marketing and their use of market research in refining the product offer. However, until they accept that this augmented brand approach is at best a partial interpretation of customer value, they will not be free to look for total customer solutions. Customer value and brand value can be aligned using UOVP methodologies

> *Without the mechanism for continuous alignment, brand value ceases to be the embodiment of customer value*

and a total solution developed by the UOVP architect. We would like to see marketing management lead this alignment by aspiring to become the UOVP architects.

This role is fundamentally different from managing product brands in terms of responsibilities, scope, and content. The mandate and responsibilities are outlined next so as to identify the new skills needed by marketers to fulfil the role effectively.

THE MANDATE AND RESPONSIBILITIES
OF THE UOVP ARCHITECT

Suggested guidelines for the UOVP architect

Ability to commit to customers and suppliers

To create customer value by working within a network of organizations, individuals must be empowered to make commitments for the
organization. If no one can do so, customers and business partners
will not find it easy to work with the organization as it falls back into
the sequential processing of information that inhibits breakthrough
improvements. The virtuous circle of UOVP brand building will be to
measure customer and organization brand value and manage the gap
between them. This will involve the architect working with the organization's process owners, suppliers, customers and potential alliance
partners.

Build and lead a network of alliances

As the interdependency between companies in the value chain
increases and reputations become intertwined, it is in everyone's
interest to ensure that customers perceive and receive a UOVP that is
seamlessly intertwined in each of its customer-facing activities.
Aligned values, co-branding, reputation management and shared customers are becoming the context of organization brand management;
who is better positioned than marketing management to grow into
this role?

Process management must deliver against the UOVP

In this book, we have adopted five core processes to represent how
customer value is delivered through the UOVP architecture. Some
organizations may decide that they have different core processes to

these or, indeed, choose to manage a greater number. The UOVP architect plays a major role in building a team from the individual process owners, ensuring trade-offs between individual processes are made in consideration of the overall customer proposition. The architect also works with process owners to facilitate closer relationships with customers, suppliers and potential alliance partners. While process owners will build many of these relationships through their own initiatives, ultimately, someone must facilitate their integration. If not, companies may only succeed in replacing functional silos with process ones.

Ensure access to marketing capabilities

Excellence in the tasks of marketing at a product level is still necessary. There will still be a need for research design and interpretation, advertising, promotion and publicity. Companies with a portfolio of product brands will still need excellent brand management. Process management of customer value creation cannot be an excuse for

> *The true-blue marketers of today need to be willing to learn additional skills and develop broader business interests to become the UOVP leaders of tomorrow*

"shared ignorance" replacing expert and informed marketers. Whether or not these capabilities are provided in-house or externally, the organization needs a group of people who will ensure that process owners get the right capabilities from people who are also able to judge quality. The increased priority for the organization brand name in the UOVP methodology also mandates that the classical marketing programs still utilized is of the very best quality; many companies will only have one brand with which to experiment.

Team involvement and commitment

This means that the true-blue marketers of today need to be willing to learn additional skills and develop broader business interests to become the UOVP leaders of tomorrow. These multiple skills range from team management to financial literacy. Value chain differentiation will become the hallmark of successful UOVP management as marketers progress from their stock-in-trade of 4Ps marketing. Too narrow a definition of marketing will produce too narrow a UOVP architecture in response.

The activities of the UOVP architect

By returning to the planning process outlined in Chapter 4, we can map out a new "job description" for marketing leaders and demonstrate that, in so doing, we create a virtuous circle of added value that maps the new manner in which marketers will build brands (Fig. 10.1).

The tasks of the UOVP architect can be integrated into the stages of UOVP planning and management and is concerned with four deliverables as identified in the figure.

Customer value statement
A statement of what creates customer value in your market(s) now and in the future. It is created through value analysis which develops a profound understanding of the value drivers in the market. The value analysis procedures include a thorough review of the environment, the customers' business, scenario modelling and pure imagination of what could be. The work incorporates fact-driven, analytical thinking with intuition, creativity and imagination. It must involve the customer, industry experts, outside agent provocateurs as well company executives for it to be sufficiently credible to lead internal changes that follow.

The UOVP architecture
The cable and wires diagram for your organization is developed

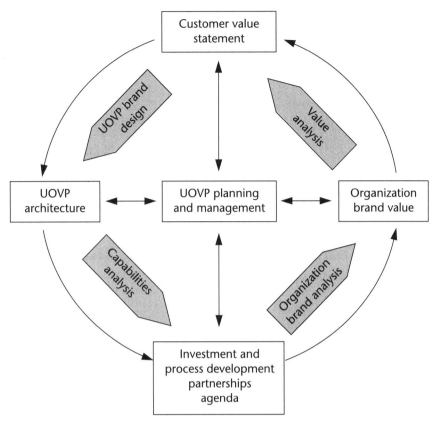

Fig. 10.1 The virtuous circle of UOVP brand building

through UOVP brand design. The UOVP brand design creates the right mix of the four key variables of reputation, performance, portfolio (product brands and customers) and networks. This mix must be made in consideration of customer value and competitors. The brand design also creates the "width" of each process wire, providing a blueprint for process management and development. This latter part of brand design is naturally done as a collaborative effort with the process owners. The procedures at this stage for the UOVP architect will vary according to circumstance. However, there is a strong probability that they will include analysis as well as cross-process workshops.

The investment, process development and partnerships agenda

This is a statement of how the organization will secure the capabilities it needs to implement the UOVP architecture. So far, the work of UOVP brand building has been "demand" focused, looking at creating customer value and the processes needed to delivery it. It is at this stage that the UOVP architect must integrate the capabilities of the organization with the blueprint. To identify the gaps, procedures at this stage include a capabilities audit, benchmarking, and third-party assessment. Where there are capabilities gaps, the company must decide whether to develop them in-house or through some sort of collaborative effort with other companies.

The agenda will outline which capabilities are to be developed within the organization and which will be sourced through other companies. Against each, there will be a plan for how those capabilities are to be developed, the governance of alliances and partnerships and the appropriate benchmarks and measures (so that the organization knows what has been achieved).

Statement of the organization's brand value

This is an estimate of the strength and meaning of the organization's name among its key audiences and a statement of how it will be built upon in the future. The purpose of this deliverable is to provide a tangible measure of success or failure of the new brand. The arguments for producing this are somewhat analogous to those used for putting brands on the balance sheet; you do not manage what you do not measure. However, the narrowing of the value gap need not be held hostage to a resolution of the brands-on-the-balance-sheet issue. The statement is produced from an organization brand analysis whose procedures include benchmarking, market research, external interviews, and creative workshops. One of the most important aspects to this analysis is the inclusion of capability owners (internal and external) to influence the direction of brand value. In line with our view of

Level 4 partnerships in the supply partnership chapter, external partners' capabilities can propel the brand into new areas of added value which should build a much more powerful UOVP than that achievable from internal resources alone.

THE REHABILITATED MARKETER

The new role of marketing management is to build a much deeper understanding of customer value and to create the relevant customer proposition by aligning the organization's core processes. This means ensuring that the capabilities needed to deliver the proposition are available to the process owners and the entire value network increases brand value (hence customer value) year on year.

The aligning of the organization to its external environment has always been the very broadest mandate of marketing. In order to accomplish this task, marketing management developed methodologies and tools that integrated the functional organization to create product brands that met the needs of the external environment. The world in which marketing management now operates has undergone a radical transformation in the 1990s, yet the methodologies and tools have remained largely unchanged. This has significantly contributed to the gap between brand and customer value and is the *cri de coeur* of our book.

SUMMARY

Marketing management should not confuse the ends with the means. Marketers must relegate the comfortable and familiar to its proper place and embrace new methodologies designed for the modern, process-centered organization and emerging customer

demands. We believe that the UOVP is the most promising new methodology for this task as it offers a number of tools with which marketers can bridge the value gap and return them to their place at the heart of value adding activities.

INDEX